Coors: A Rocky Mountain Legend

COORS

A Rocky Mountain Legend

Russ Banham

GREENWICH PUBLISHING GROUP, INC.
LYME, CONNECTICUT

Produced and published by Greenwich Publishing Group, Inc.
Lyme, Connecticut

Design by Clare Cunningham Graphic Design
Essex, Connecticut

Separation and film assembly by Silver Eagle Graphics, Inc.

Library of Congress Catalog Card Number: 97-81376

ISBN: 0-944641-29-6

First Printing: February 1998

10 9 8 7 6 5 4 3 2

The following are current or former trademarks of Coors Brewing Company:

A. Coors (signature), Banquet, Blue Moon, the Castle Rock logo, Coors Artic Ice, Coors Cutter, Coors Dry, Coors Export Lager, Coors Extra Gold, Coors Light, Coors Non-Alcoholic, George Killian's Irish Honey, George Killian's Irish Red, Herman Joseph's, Keystone Light, Original Coors, Party Ball, The SandLot Brewery, The Silver Bullet, Winterfest, Zima, "America's Fine Light Beer" slogan, "Killian's Red" slogan, "Tap the Rockies."

Photography Credits:
All images and artifacts pictured in the book appear courtesy of Coors Brewing Company except the following images: p. 11 (lower right), p. 31 (lower right), p. 36 (lower left), p. 39 (lower right), p. 41 (lower right), p. 42 (lower right), p. 44 (lower left), p. 49 (middle right), p. 51 (top), p. 64, p. 65 (bottom), p. 68 (upper and lower right), p. 91 (bottom), p. 95 (inset), p. 106 (both bottom right), which appear courtesy of Brad Baker. The clip on p. 61 (right) ©Copyrighted Chicago Tribune Company. All rights reserved. Used with permission. The photo on p. 61 (right) appears courtesy AP/Wide World Photos. Page 85 (bottom) is reprinted with permission of The Denver Post.

Photography of Coors artifacts by Brian Payne

TABLE OF CONTENTS

PROLOGUE

Why do some people consider it a sin to be a conservative and not a sin to be a liberal?" Bill Coors asks with a wry expression in our first interview. It was a typically hot, sunny June day in Golden, Colorado, home to the international beer company built by Coors' grandfather, Adolph Coors, 125 years ago.

Bill (he prefers everyone to call him by his first name, be they foreign dignitaries or employees on Coors' bottle line) sat comfortably in his modest office in an open collar shirt and a pair of khakis. Fit as a fiddle, with a mind twice as nimble as executives half his age, he looked decades younger than his 80 years.

Like all good rhetorical questions, this one spoke volumes. To the public, Adolph Coors Company is a dichotomy, renowned for the exceptional quality of its beer, but once censured by some groups for the conservative political views of the Coors family. This image of the Coors family as a band of intolerant right-wingers isolated in the Colorado mountains is rather widespread, a testament to the effectiveness of an AFL-CIO smear campaign in the late 1970s. Coors' union problems prompted the attack, which spawned a devastating boycott by several interest groups. Although the company later made amends with these organizations and today is routinely praised for its minority hiring programs, environmental activism and social agenda, it has been unable to entirely shake this right-wing image.

That's too bad, for the family's conservative principles — a strong work ethic, a passion for excellence and a firm belief in the free market system — are the bedrock upon which the company was built. Passed down from generation to generation, these ideals guided Coors from a tiny brewery in the Colorado foothills into what is now the third-largest beer company in America and the ninth-largest in the world.

While Bill Coors considers himself a conservative, gluing such a label on him belies his complexity as a human being. Despite great personal wealth, he lives modestly, remains frugal and even shops at the local store for Coors beer. Considered a "straight arrow," he favors parental leave and drug decriminalization measures, practices transcendental meditation and plays ragtime and jazz music on the piano. Although colleagues say he is quiet and almost shy, he eloquently championed free speech in a 1984 address at Harvard University. He's one of the oldest individuals ever to climb Mount Kilimanjaro, despite a childhood bicycle injury that left him unable to play many sports.

Ask people who have worked with Bill Coors for a character reference and they invariably cite his intelligence, compassion, sensitivity and insight — not his political views. He is one of a few octogenarians still working every day, and one of only a handful bearing the title chairman.

Bill Coors' life and memories span the entire history of the Coors Brewing Company. He has avid memories of his grandfather and father, Adolph Jr., the company's two previous chairmen. Today he works closely with his nephews — Pete, Joe Jr. and Jeff — running the various Coors enterprises.

Each chapter of this book is interspersed with his reminiscences. And to him, this book is dedicated.

At the turn of the century, Coors Lake and Golden Grove were the scene of many afternoon picnics and leisurely promenades. Here, Adolph Coors, Sr., walks with his grandsons — Adolph III, Bill and Joe — and their cousin, John Potter.

CHAPTER ONE

CLEAR

AMBITION

I n the formal dining room of the mansion built by his grandfather more than a century ago — a house packed with a million memories and stories — Bill Coors, his eyes squinting to better "see" the past, reminisced about the remarkable life of Adolph Coors and the company he founded.

"My grandfather used to sit right here where I'm sitting at the head of this table during the family's weekly Sunday dinner," the 80-year-old patriarch recalled.

"My brothers, Ad and Joe, and I used to sit at a smaller table by the alcove. Grandfather would carve the turkey, and all the adults got served first while we little kids sat there and waited, our eyes big as saucers.

"Tradition was important to him. Like my father, my grandfather was a fairly rigid man. He brooked no deviation from the straight and narrow. He had what we would call today a code of ethics. Right was right and wrong was wrong. He also had something many would consider a rare trait — a certainty about who he was and what he needed to accomplish.

Adolph Coors, seen here during the trying last years of his life, was gifted with intense ambition and the grit to accomplish his goals. Although modest in height, Coors was a giant in every sense of the word. Fellow businessmen admired his tenacity and employees adored him.

"His family was his world, and every member better measure up or else. He also was a private, contemplative person. At Sunday dinner in the summertime, he'd have this little split of Rhine wine, and after dinner he'd go outside and sit in a wicker chair under this old ironwood tree and smoke a cigar, alone with his thoughts. Perhaps he thought of his life as a boy in Germany, or of his early days in Colorado, when it was still the Wild West. I never inquired, and he never offered.

"Grandfather also was a very courageous man. He overcame obstacles in his life that would have toppled most people. He was orphaned at 15, in Germany, in the late 1860s — a time of tremendous repression and strife with Austria. To escape, he stowed on board a ship bound for America at the tender age of 21, without a penny in his pocket or knowing a lick of English. They wanted to turn him back when he got here, but he was able to convince them otherwise.

"What did my grandfather believe in? I guess, above all, in the promise of the individual. Unlike Germany, where a king ruled and a class structure dominated, America was a place where a man mattered more than the state — a land where no man had to bow. In America, a man could stand up free of bloodlines and become what he wanted to become. And my grandfather took flight for this freedom."

The life of Adolph Coors is the life of an American legend — a mythic, yet true, account of a penniless immigrant finding fame and fortune in America, his adopted land. It is a story of personal ambition, courage and determination against tremendous odds, and by extension, of a country in which every man has a shot at greatness. Mostly, it is about one man who never let go of his vision — even when all appeared lost.

Adolph Coors was born February 4, 1847, the first child of Joseph and Helene Coors in an area of Germany just south of Holland that today is called Wuppertal-Oberbarmen. The family moved a year later from this rolling hill country to the flatlands of Dortmund, a thriving industrial city where Adolph's father, a master miller, found work as a supervisor in a steam-powered mill.

Like many boys, Adolph learned several trades, including flour miller, printer and book binder, but his father pointed him in another direction — the brewery business. Joseph Coors had contacts at the famous Wenker Brewery across the street from the Coors home, and after finishing grammar school, Adolph was enrolled there as a business apprentice. He was 14 years old.

Tragedy struck in April 1862, when tuberculosis claimed the life of Adolph's mother. Eight months later, his father also died, and he and his younger siblings, William and Helene, were taken in by a local Catholic orphanage.

His guardian influenced him to move from the brewery's commercial side to the technical side, where the earning potential was higher. The timing was excellent. Wenker was converting from manual brewing to industrial production using steam engines, and Adolph experienced this progressive development firsthand.

At the age of 21, Adolph was subject to conscription in the Prussian army. Fresh in his memory were impressions of the bloody Austro-Prussian war of 1866, and the threat of ongoing conflict. "He concluded either he had to serve the king or leave the country," reads an 1880 biography. He chose the latter.

Like a half-million other Germans who had emigrated to America between 1866 and 1879, Coors had a compelling belief in the promise of the New World, a land of freedom reputed to offer unlimited opportunity to individuals with initiative and a talent for hard work. Yet, he realized if he emigrated to the United States, he risked not seeing his brother or sister again.

An intense desire for freedom and the spiritual inheritance from his forefathers — miller folk were often said to be possessed of wanderlust — finally overcame all doubts. In 1868, Adolph Coors set sail for the New World.

TENACITY AND THRIFT

He made his way first to Hamburg, where he stowed on board a ship bound for the United States. Halfway across the Atlantic, however, the ship's crew discovered him hiding in steerage. Adolph's English was poor and he had no money, yet upon arrival in Baltimore, he convinced the port authorities to grant him a grace period to pay off his passage. Within a year, he covered his debts, found steady work and opened a bank account.

Gradually, he made his way west. He earned as he travelled, trying his hand as a bricklayer, stone cutter, fireman and hoisting engineer doing pick and shovel work on the Chicago Drainage Canal. Then, in August 1869, he re-entered the beer business, taking a position at the Stenger Brewery in Naperville, Illinois.

John Stenger, the brewery's proprietor, took an immediate liking to Adolph and envisioned in him a potential husband for one of his three daughters. Apparently not intrigued with the prospect, Coors resigned in January 1872 and continued his west-

ward journey on the recently completed transcontinental railroad. He arrived in Denver, Colorado, a rugged, 14-year-old city teeming with opportunity.

His first month there he worked as a gardener, an avocation that became a lifelong passion. Then, on May 1, 1872, having saved his meager earnings over the years, he purchased a partnership in the bottling business of John Staderman. Before the year was out, Coors was the sole proprietor. An 1873 advertisement described him as a dealer in "bottled beer, ale, porter and cider, imported and domestic wines, and seltzer water."

Although the bottling business was successful, the young man had bigger plans. On his Sundays off, he surveyed the foothills west of Denver looking for a suitable location to build a brewery. He was captivated by the rich Clear Creek valley east of Golden, where cool, crystalline springs bubbled over in abundance among the willows. On the banks of the creek, he discovered an abandoned brick and stone tannery and judged it a perfect site for a brewery. "My grandfather always said the most important ingredient in beer is water," Bill Coors says.

"So while others here searched for gold, he searched for treasure of a different kind — a high-quality and reliable supply of water." Though Coors' ambition was bountiful, his funds were not. Serendipity intervened in the form of Jacob Schueler, the

The Golden Brewery's first beer, Golden Lager, was an instant success. Rather than rely on others to malt its barley — the common practice at competing breweries — the brewery did all its own malting on-site. The beer's quality, thus, was consistent and reliable.

Every entrepreneur needs an "angel" — a venture capitalist who believes in the dream. Jacob Schueler, a prosperous Denverite, filled this role for Adolph Coors, investing $18,000 (to Coors' $2,000) to launch the Golden Brewery.

prosperous owner of a Denver confectionery and ice cream parlor and one of Coors' better bottling customers. Impressed with the young German's enthusiasm and his 11 years of experience as a brewer, Schueler agreed to finance his plans.

Coors sold the bottling business in October 1873 and invested $2,000, along with Schueler's $18,000, in developing the Golden Brewery. The partners spent $2,500 to buy the six-year-old tannery and an odd-shaped section of land less than 250 by 500 feet. The remainder of their investment was spent to convert it into a brewery. This venture would be the foundation of Coors Brewing Company.

TOUGH TIMES IN A TOUGH TOWN

They could not have picked a worse time to start a new business. The failure of several eastern banks in 1873 tightened money conditions nationwide. All railroad enterprises stopped dead in their tracks, and a recent grasshopper plague in the Territory of Colorado decimated area crops. The partners also entered a highly competitive field. There were seven local breweries in Denver, a city with barely 50,000 people.

But Coors had gumption and a solid business strategy. Unlike other breweries, his would be a self-reliant company, one controlling as many variables as possible involved in the process of producing and selling beer. This philosophy eventually became the motto of the company: "The more we do ourselves, the higher quality we have."

His strategy also called for the brewery to expand as business grew — paid for not by bank loans but through retained earnings. Most importantly, the brewery would make the best darn beer possible, using only the finest ingredients, modern equipment and immaculate brewing conditions.

Schueler & Coors' first beer — Golden Lager — hit the market in the first months of 1874. By April more than 100 eight-gallon kegs a day were being produced, packaged in hand-made, solid oak barrels for sale in Golden and nearby mining towns. The beer was an instant success — the brewery turned a profit in less than a year, selling more than 3,500 barrels in the first 12 months of operation. With all those breweries around, Coors must have been doing something right.

Indeed, the Golden Brewery "occupies the best location in Colorado, commands a full supply of pure water, and has the further advantage of railroad communications with the mining districts," reported the *Colorado Transcript*, a local newspaper.

Since Golden was the

*W*hen Coors started the Golden Brewery in 1873, Colorado wasn't even a state. Buffalo roamed the plains and six-gun justice ruled the territory.

LONGMONT SEP 6 1888 COLO

U.S. POSTAGE 3 THREE CENTS 3

ADOLPH COORS,
--SUCCESSOR TO--
CHUELER & COORS,
Brewers of Golden Lager Beer,
GOLDEN, COLO.

Very Strange Houseguest, Indeed

The Coors mansion is duly recognized as one of Colorado's premier historical homes, an ornate masterpiece of European craftsmanship amid the bustling industrial landscape of the world's largest brewery.

The house, which served as the original home of Adolph Coors and is occasionally used by the Coors family for business luncheons, also had its more, shall we say, practical purposes. In the 1920s, Adolph and Louisa Coors used two rooms of the mansion to store barley. The founder even requested an insurance rate reduction for the rooms, since they were used for business purposes. It is unknown whether the insurance company agreed.

Apparently, Louisa was less than pleased with the arrangement, especially when one wall collapsed, sending tons of barley into the lavish home! "She held her temper, but I'm sure Grandfather sensed her displeasure," Bill Coors recalls. From then on, the barley was stored at the brewery.

The brewery grew rapidly in its first dozen years. Profits were invested in new equipment and facilities, including a two-story cleaning house for washing kegs, a bottling house and a coopers' shop for building barrels.

"Gateway to Mining," word of the beer's taste and quality spread quickly from mining camp to mining camp. Distribution was aided by Golden's location on the Colorado Central Railroad, just north across Clear Creek from the brewery. Off the railcar, wagonloads of beer were pulled by mules to thirsty miners in the foothills.

The fledgling company took out its first advertisement in the *Transcript* in July 1874. It was succinct, stating simply:

GOLDEN BREWERY
Schuler (sic) & Coors, Prop'rs
Golden, Colorado

Business grew fast, especially in Denver, where Golden Lager was a hit. As planned, Coors and Schueler reinvested their profits into the brewery's expansion, completing extensive remodeling in

late 1874. They installed state-of-the-art steam pumps, a malt mill and mash tub, a storeroom for malt and hops and a water tank capable of holding 90 barrels.

In addition, a wooden icehouse capable of holding 1,500 tons of ice was built over the brewery's new stone fermenting cellars. Ice was cut from nearby ponds in winter, placed in straw and sawdust and delivered by wagon to the icehouse, as well as throughout Golden for sale to local businesses. The price was 40 cents for 100 pounds.

Expansion continued in 1875. The brewery employed 35 men to build a bottling facility and malt house, the former to avoid the high prices of Eastern glassmakers and the latter as a quality control measure. The workers also constructed an ice dam over Clear Creek for its burgeoning ice business and a pavilion near a grove of willows for social activities. Called Golden Grove, it would become the scene of many lively gatherings in the Victorian era.

"Manufacturer of the Purest Article"

It was a spirited time to be living in the frontier West. Millions of buffalo still roamed the eastern plains of territorial Colorado, and skirmishes between the U.S. Cavalry and area Native Americans were common. In 1875, just 60 miles east of Colorado in Monument Station, Kansas, one battle resulted in the deaths of 27 Native Americans and two soldiers.

Colorado became a state with 135,000 citizens in 1876, triple the number of people six years earlier. As Coors' market expanded, so did its competition. Twenty-seven breweries dotted the state in 1878, up from 18 in 1875. The Golden Brewery met the pressure head on, reaching beyond Colorado to the territories of New Mexico, Wyoming and Utah, and the states of Nevada, California, Kansas and Nebraska. The new distribution outlets motivated the company's first marketing theme — "Bottling for Export a Specealty [sic]."

Over the years, the ever-frugal Coors saved his money and gradually bought out Schueler's investment. In May 1880, he was at last the sole proprietor of the Golden Brewery. He also married. On April 12, 1879, in a quiet ceremony performed in the home he had built on brewery grounds, "the popular and successful brewer," the *Transcript* reported, married Miss Louisa Weber of Denver. Together, they would raise six children — three sons and three daughters.

A local historian wrote in 1880 that Adolph Coors had become "one of the successful merchants of the city of Golden, priding himself as a manufacturer of the purest article, in his branch of the business, now on the market."

That was just the beginning.

"No Shade of Adulteration"

The population of Colorado skyrocketed to nearly 200,000 in 1880. The Golden Brewery reflected the upturn, selling more than 4,000 barrels that year. Coors planned further expansion projects on a drawing board he kept handy in his office. "He liked to see things built," Bill Coors says. "And when they weren't built the way he wanted them to be, he had them torn down and rebuilt."

In 1884, a three-story beer storage facility was constructed. Other additions included a two-story cleaning house for washing kegs and a coopers' shop for building barrels. New equipment was purchased, including a bottle washer and a patent corking machine. The latter closed bottles with a cork covered in foil and wire, much like the champagne bottles of today. Coors hired "the best trained

Adolph Coors and Louisa Weber, seen above on their wedding day in 1879 and below, were a traditional German husband and wife. He ran the family business, and she reared their children — three sons and three daughters. Both lived well into their seventies and saw the succeeding generations leave their mark on the company.

Pigeonholing a Kid

Ken Golightly finished his career with Coors in 1977 evaluating and selecting new distributors in the company's growing marketing region. His beginnings with the company also required an expert eye. "When I was 11 years old, Adolph Coors hired me to shoot any pigeons I could find at the plant," Ken recalls.

"There were two things Mr. Coors hated — pigeons and black smoke coming out of the smokestack. The latter meant fuel was burning up, and that was a waste. The former, well, he put a high price on cleanliness. He pretty much hated pigeons for all the obvious reasons.

"My father was Golden's policeman and he and Mr. Coors got to talking one day about how I was such an awful good shot. I was selling newspapers at the time for $9 a month, when Mr. Coors said he would supply me with ammunition — BBs, really — to kill pigeons at a nickel a head. Well, there were plenty of pigeons around. I quit my paper route quickly.

"There was one hitch to our agreement, though. For every pigeon I shot that died on the roof of a building, I had to pay Mr. Coors 25 cents. You see, he didn't want the pigeons stuck up there. Anyway, that kind of money was incentive enough: I never had to pay him a penny."

men he could find" to build his buildings and brew his beer, the *Transcript* reported. Photos from the period show powerfully built workers in polished black leather boots that rose up above their knees. Nearly all were of German heritage, and German was the predominant language spoken at the brewery.

A welcome face among the new workers was Coors' brother William, who emigrated to the U.S. as well and was brought to Golden in late 1880 to become superintendent of the bottling department. Two years later, the bottle-making plant was closed, and William became the company's representative in Denver.

Driving the plant closure was pure economics: Empty bottles were being resold by junk dealers at one-quarter the price the company charged

for new ones. Coors took another shot at the bottle-making business in 1886, incorporating the Colorado Glass Works with other prominent Goldenites. Glass blowers were recruited from Ohio and Illinois to manufacture bottles for the brewery and for general sale. Unfortunately, the men were heavy drinkers and unwilling to work steadily. The plant was shut down by a strike after only 18 months of operation.

Business at the brewery was another matter,

Adolph Coors preferred to control as many variables as possible in the manufacturing of beer, including bottling. The Colorado Glass Works, Coors' early bottling enterprise, lost out to junk dealers who resold empty bottles at one-quarter the price of Coors' new ones. In 1885, Coors decided it was better business to buy back used beer bottles at 45 cents for a dozen — the first of many recycling efforts.

nearly doubling between 1882 and 1883. Two new brews were added: Coors Export Beer and Pilsener Lager Beer (with the old style spelling), sold both in kegs and bottles. To reinforce the salutary image of his beers, Coors drew upon the nearby Table Mountains, incorporating an illustration of Castle Rock on company letterheads as early as 1884. Ten years later, the Castle Rock illustration would be used for the first time in a newspaper advertisement. It remains the company's trademark today.

Many local publications touted the "superior quality" of Golden beer, "the excellence of the materials used" and "the purity of the water." The *Globe*, Golden's local paper, reported "no shade of adulteration in it," adding in another article that the brewery was "as clean as the parlour of your home." These testimonials drew consumers by the wagonload to the brewery's doorstep, where a small retail business flourished.

Families would send their sons to the brewery with a wooden bucket lined in lard, to take home a fresh, ice-cold bucket of beer for supper. The lard kept the bucket from leaking, and there would be less foam and therefore more beer for the family supper. This practice was known as "rushing the growler."

In 1886, Coors turned the retailing over to a Golden storekeeper, Julius Schultz, who promised to deliver beer "free of charge at the same rate heretofore charged at the brewery." Schultz received orders at his shop — the first time Coors was sold in a store.

Business rose steadily, and in 1887 — the year electric lights came to Golden — more than 7,000 barrels of beer were sold. A scant three years later, as the state's population topped 400,000, the brewery sold 17,600 barrels. Adolph Coors became known as "the millionaire brewer of Colorado."

Once again, he poured his profits into expansion. To augment ice capacity from Clear Creek, the company constructed its first artificial ice plant in 1890. New bottling machinery was purchased following the invention of the crown crimped cap in 1892. And more land was bought; upon it

Coors bottled beer travelled beyond Colorado to neighboring states, prompting the company's first advertising theme: "Bottling for Export a Speceally [sic]." Plaques like the one above were displayed at brewery-owned distribution outlets throughout Colorado.

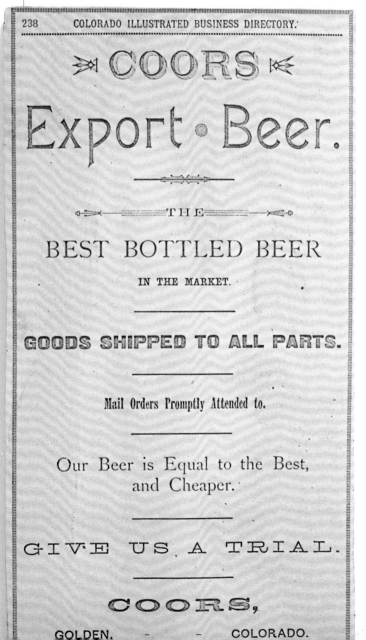

238   COLORADO ILLUSTRATED BUSINESS DIRECTORY.

⤜ COORS ⤛
Export · Beer.

THE

BEST BOTTLED BEER

IN THE MARKET.

GOODS SHIPPED TO ALL PARTS.

Mail Orders Promptly Attended to.

Our Beer is Equal to the Best, and Cheaper.

GIVE US A TRIAL.

COORS,

GOLDEN.   -   COLORADO.

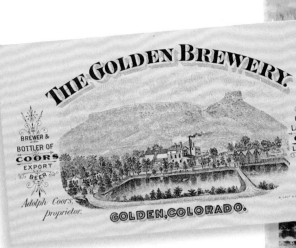

Adolph Coors was determined to humanize the industrial vista of a brewery. He had two lakes constructed and surrounded them with trees. Coors' early advertising focused on natural scenes and landscapes like those that surrounded the brewery. The larger picture underscores the importance of the railroad to the fledgling company's distribution plan. Coors Export Beer was introduced expressly for distribution outside Golden.

Coors would build Golden's first "skyscraper" — a seven-story building — in 1895.

Revised federal tax laws in 1890 boosted Coors' sale of bottled beer. Previously, beer had to be barreled with tax stamps prior to bottling — a time-consuming and laborious process. Beer now could be taxed by liquid meters in pipes between the brewery and bottle house, removing the need for it to be prekegged. Within a year, more than one-third of Coors' output was bottled.

A new electric railroad connecting Golden to Denver in 1893 eased distribution, prodding Coors to enhance advertising in the capital city.

Calendars with artwork featuring female figures — Coors' first illustrated ads — were distributed that year. The brewery also sent an elaborate float to the first Denver Mountain and Plain Festival in 1895 and for several years thereafter. Coors "never does anything by halves," a local paper reported.

Although Denver was the company's largest market, the city was only one of its 15 Colorado-based agencies and depots. Others included Pueblo, Trinidad, Colorado Springs, Aspen and Fort Collins. Beer was shipped by rail to the depots and stored in company-owned warehouses, which had large double doors to allow a horse-

Castle Rock was used
on company letterhead
as early as 1884, and
eventually became the
brewery's predominant
advertising logo. As the
company expanded
over the years, the
connection to the
Rockies and Golden

Bock beer, celebrating the imminent arrival of spring, is a German tradition dating back centuries. In 1894, the *Colorado Transcript* reported that "Adolph Coors' Bock beer is ripe and is pronounced a first class article by connoisseurs."

Coors followed the tradition in the early twentieth century of using female figures in its artwork, especially on the covers of early illustrated calendars.

Adolph Coors (seen here in a white hat in the second row) treated fellow workers at the brewery like members of an extended family. Flanking the beer case in the front row are the founder's young sons, Grover (left) and Herman. The men along the top left carrying buggy whips were the "teamsters" who drove Coors' horse-drawn wagons up the mountain. The men along the top right holding "turning pads" were "maltsters." Many workers joined the local chapter of the newly formed union of United Brewery Workmen.

1894.

NATIONAL UNION OF THE
United Brewery Workmen
— OF THE —
UNITED STATES,
LOCAL UNION No. 44.
Denver, Colo.

National Union of The United Brewery Workmen
ORGANIZED
AUG. 29TH 1886
Of The United States.

Card of Membership.
Herzel, Wilhelm
No. 36.
Secretary

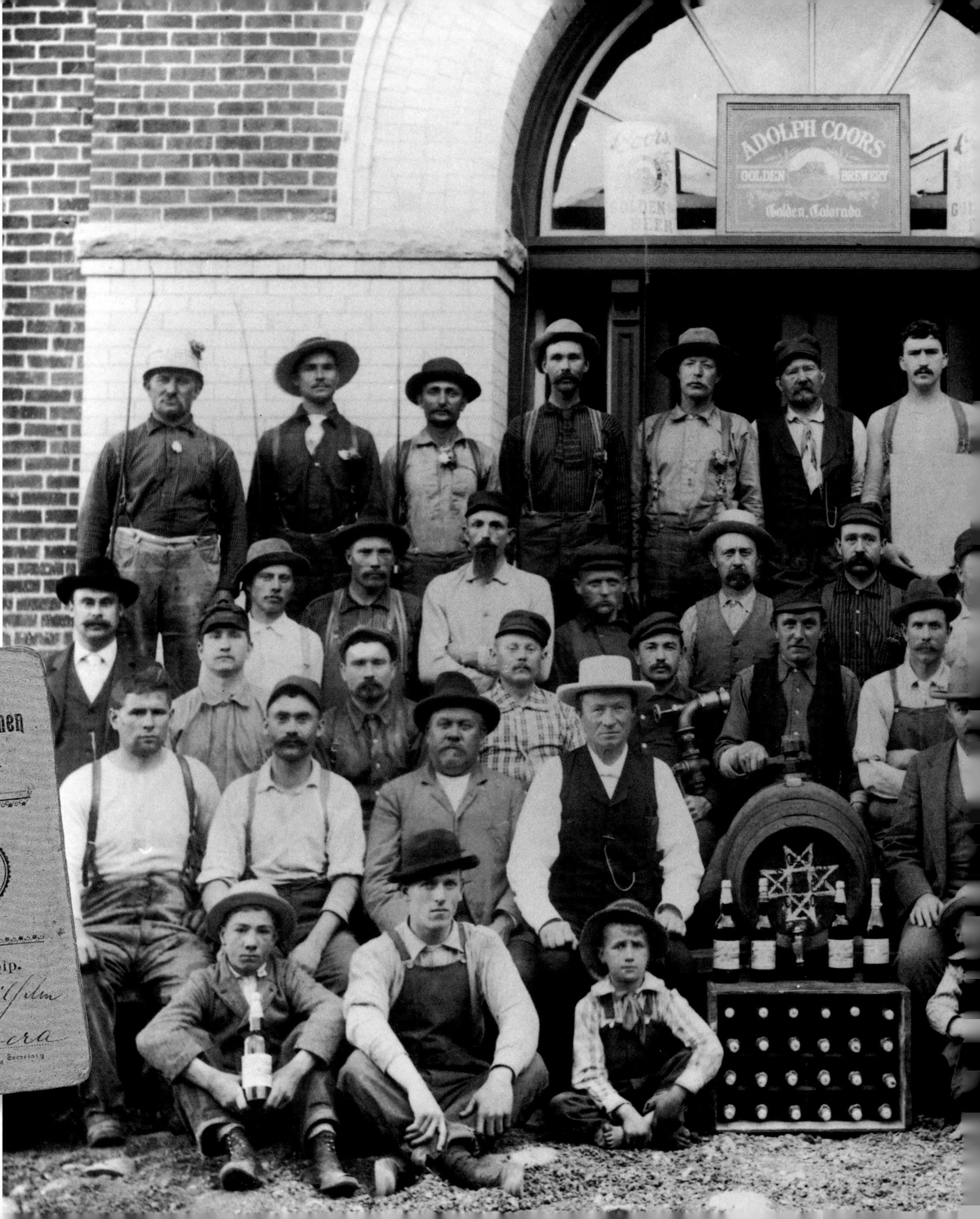

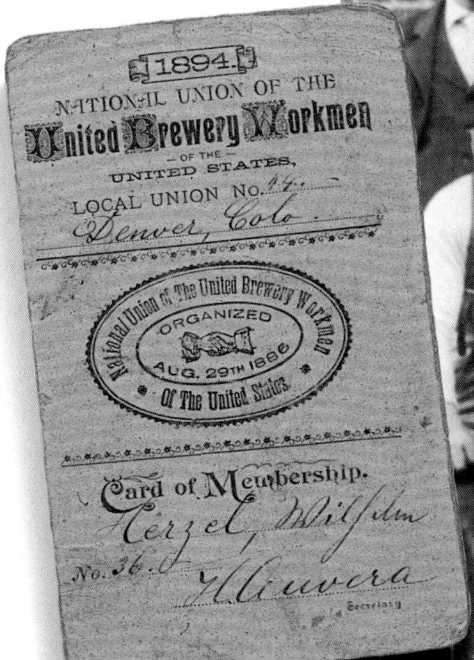

drawn wagon to be pulled in and loaded. For the most part, the beer was shipped in kegs and wholesalers did their own bottling — by hand.

In September 1893, Coors brought his beers to the Chicago World's Fair to compete against the products of 25 other American and several foreign breweries. Coors won an award for brilliancy, flavor, chemical analysis and commercial flavor and was the only winner west of the Missouri.

As the Coors family's prosperity — and numbers — enlarged, they moved from their modest home in 1890 into the "big house," a residence that incorporated the old Golden Grove pavilion structure. No sooner had they settled in, however, when financial war clouds gathered on the horizon.

The Panic of 1893, the country's worst depression at the time, forced the closure of more than a dozen Denver area banks. Unemployment soared, and several "unfortunates" could be seen "with all sorts of appliances" scouring Clear Creek for gold, the *Transcript* reported. Beer production plunged — of the 23 breweries open in the state for business in 1893, only 16 remained three years later.

The Golden Brewery weathered the financial storm better than most, and its output dipped only slightly. A brief work stoppage by employees was settled when Coors agreed to a nine-hour workday at the same pay employees previously received for 10 hours. He also gave them a five-minute break each hour, during which "beer boys" filled their copper mugs with free brew.

More threatening, however, was the Great Memorial Day Flood of 1894, which destroyed a newly completed addition to the brewery and carried away two large ice reservoirs. The Coors family home was surrounded by the floodwaters and had to be abandoned for a short period. Adolph Coors acted quickly, purchasing lots on the opposite side of the creek and putting "an army of men [to] work…to turn the channel

In 1893 Adolph Coors travelled to the Chicago Exposition to enter Coors beer in a contest against other breweries. The plaque above was presented to Coors awarding its beers top prize for brilliancy and flavor, among other accolades.

THE COORS MANSION

In the heart of the industrial landscape that is the largest brewery in the world sits a living monument to its heritage — the fabled Coors mansion built by Adolph Coors as a present to his wife, Louisa, in 1890. The Victorian-era home is a blend of Ornate Queen Anne architectural design and the more utilitarian tastes of the company's founder. Coors previously owned a dance pavilion and beer garden on the site, which had closed years before. From the remains of the pavilion he erected the "big house," as the Coors family members called it then and continue to call it today.

The residence is the sole survivor of three family cottages built on the brewery grounds over the past 125 years. The others — inhabited by various Coors family members — were torn down to accommodate plant expansion. In 1894, the mansion was nearly destroyed by the Great Memorial Day Flood. Coors hired dozens of men to divert the flood waters before they reached his home.

Originally, the mansion was the centerpiece of Coors' lavish gardens and outbuildings, the latter housing a bowling alley, pool and small gymnasium. A greenhouse to furnish year-round flowers for nearby offices was a part of this magnificent menagerie and remains standing. Gardening was

Although the gracious living room seen here has dark moldings, the woodworking in other rooms is bleached white. Bill Coors explains why. "My mother hired some men to bleach all the oak moldings, the style of the day. Had my father not gotten home in time to stop her, she might have bleached the whole house!" Suffice it to say, the moldings are gorgeous in any color.

Adolph Coors' passion.

Bill Coors has a special fondness for the big house. "I was born in one of the cottages and lived there until 1934, when my parents moved to the mansion," the company's chairman recalls. "It was originally a temporary move. My parents planned to recreate their cottage atop the brewery, but instead, they lived at the mansion until their deaths in 1970."

Ironically, an elevator built to transport the family to the contemplated cottage apartment remains, its tight confines a mystery to the many brewery visitors that use it today.

The Coors mansion was moved from its original location — about 450 feet from its present site — in 1962 to further the expansion of the brewery and accommodate a better view of the Table Mountains. It has been meticulously maintained and is still used today by the Coors family for occasional family business lunches.

Castle Rock looms like a sentry above the rapidly expanding brewery. The seven-story structure in the center of the photo was Golden's first "skyscraper," built in 1895.

Flood Protection

In the early days, Coors beer was shipped on stage lines or on the narrow- and standard-gauge railroad lines from the brewery to Durango, Leadville, Cripple Creek and other Wild West towns in Colorado. The beer was an instant hit among thirsty miners, many of whom demanded a Golden Lager as soon as they pushed through a saloon's swinging doors.

One old letter to Adolph Coors underlines the beer's immense popularity. A tavern owner in Black Hawk ordered a railcar load of Coors beer for what he called "flood protection." Evidently, the saloonkeeper was acutely concerned that the frequent summer flash floods that threatened the Clear Creek rail line might close down the railroad and cause him a dry spell.

Either he was extremely pragmatic or very, very thirsty.

Fun and Games in the Old Days

The late Leonard Vogel, who worked at Coors from 1907 to 1973, recorded some of the more unusual after-hours activities of company employees in the early part of the century. "One time, some workers bet $5 that another brewery employee could not carry a 1/4 barrel of beer weighing about 100 pounds from the brewery up to the top of South Table Mountain and back to Coors without a rest," Vogel wrote.

"As we all watched, the man won the bet."

Another employee, he noted, once "straddled a filled hogshead weighing about 700 pounds and, with his hands, lifted it momentarily free from the floor." He, too, raked in the winnings.

Vogel also recalled another rather perilous leisure time endeavor. To traverse Clear Creek back then, employees had to walk across a three-foot-wide bridge that hung on two cables strung from Golden to East Golden. Some employees apparently liked to sway the bridge when fellow workers crossed. "One brewer lost his hold one time and got a dunking in Clear Creek, much to the mirth of the others nearby," Vogel wrote.

"It was something to see."

The Great Memorial Day Flood nearly destroyed the brewery. After the flood they moved Clear Creek into a man-made channel around the brewery to prevent another devastating flood. In digging out the channel, they found the aquifers that cool the brewing equipment.

away," the *Transcript* reported. "Every idle man in town could get work."

The losses from the flood, estimated at more than $10,000, could not have come at a worse time. Coors had just borrowed $90,000 to expand the brewery, the first time he had resorted to a loan for building purposes. Unable to pay the losses, Coors was forced to borrow yet another $90,000. "He went to the banks, and he said, 'I can't pay you. You're going to stake me again, you know. Double or nothing.' And they did," Bill Coors recalls.

"He never borrowed another dime."

THE NEW CENTURY BECKONS

As the nineteenth century drew to a close, the United States was engaged in a short war with Spain over the sinking of the battleship *Maine* in Havana harbor. Golden's volunteers in the effort included several workers from the brewery, all of whom returned home.

In those days, a job at the brewery was considered a job for life. Brewery workers earned $16 a

week for a 48-hour workweek, although bottlers got $2 less. It was enough money to cover the typical $5-a-week room and board at a Golden boarding house, with a few dollars left over for food and other necessities.

Employees' leisure activities included summer excursions into the mountains via the Colorado & Southern Railroad. Many also participated in company-sponsored sports activities, such as bowling and hockey. In 1906, the Coors bowling team defeated the C&S Railroad team.

Adolph Coors also liked bowling and had a bowling alley added to his house (not to mention a conservatory, greenhouse, indoor swimming pool and gymnasium). It's uncertain, however, if any of the company's employees actually bowled there.

It was a wondrous time, full of inventions and adventure. Electricity replaced steam as the primary source of energy in America, and the Wright brothers flew their first powered airplane. Tales of the Klondike gold rush captured the public's imagination, as did news accounts of the first Olympics in Greece, held in 1896. Automobiles began plying Golden's newly paved roads, prompting an editorial in the *Globe* urging speed limits "not greater than a fast walk."

The Golden Brewery benefited from the new technological advances. An electric power plant was installed in 1901, prompting the *Transcript* to describe the brewery as "a blaze of lights on dark nights." And the bicycle took the city by storm. "There are as many wheels in Golden in proportion to the number of people as there are in Denver," the *Transcript* reported.

The sudden popularity of bicycles alarmed the Women's Rescue League of Denver, which passed a resolution in 1895 that included an appeal to suppress bicycle riding among young women "because of the tendency to encourage immorality." While it is uncertain if Golden's female citizens heeded this advice, they were caught up in another crusade — the temperance movement.

Many Colorado women were fervent backers of alcohol prohibition initiatives, owing largely to alleged family problems caused by drunken, abusive and out-of-work husbands. As early as 1874, Golden saloon-keepers had received notices, written in "a lady's hand" and signed by the "Ladies Temperance Committee," calling for statewide prohibition. A statewide prohibition alliance was formed in Denver in 1879.

Some legislators urged giving women the right to vote in order to combat the "saloon menace." After Colorado became one of the first states in the union to approve women's suffrage in 1893, the temperance movement, in fact, gained steam. Nationally known temperance leaders visited Denver, including Carry Nation in 1906. The militant 6-foot temperance leader, bible in hand, announced, "I will rip and tear and scratch and bite and snarl and scream and roar and yell and fight until I clean this awful town up."

The temperance movement took on a quasi-religious fervor, with some organizations, such as the Anti-Saloon League of Colorado, insisting they

were "ordained by God" to force a ban on liquor. Other groups ran ads in local papers blaming alcohol for all the crimes in the statute books.

The "wets" fought back, forming the Citizens Protective Union of Colorado, of which Adolph Coors was an active member, frequently donating the use of his gardens for organizational activities and picnics. Ultimately, these efforts proved moot. City after city in the state voted to go dry, and in the November 1914 election, the state voted to make the manufacture and sale of alcoholic beverages in Colorado illegal as of January 1, 1916. Brewers were given until December 31, 1915, to dispose of their stores. That day, Coors dumped 561 barrels

The Coors family is shown above in their Sunday finery. Seated in front, from left to right, are Adolph Coors, Sr., Grover, Herman, and Louisa Coors. Standing behind are Augusta, Bertha, Louise and Adolph Coors, Jr. At left is the songbook of the "drys," as members of the growing temperance movement were called.

of beer — 17,391 gallons — into Clear Creek.

For Adolph, watching his life's work float away in the current must have been profoundly painful. Ironically, he had left Germany because of political and economic repression, and here — in this land of freedom — he had been legislated out of business.

He was almost 70 years old and had a personal wealth of some $2 million. Many people in similar circumstances would call it quits and cash in their chips — but not Adolph Coors. He felt a personal obligation to Golden to keep its citizens employed.

The signature of the founder was incorporated as the familiar trademark of Coors beer. Adolph Coors, in his office above, spent more than 50 years building up the company he founded.

He would devote all but his last days and much of his personal fortune to help Adolph Coors Brewing and Manufacturing survive the lean years of Prohibition.

And he believed in his ability to provide that. "It was not in his nature to quit," Bill Coors says. "One way or another, he would re-establish himself."

As early as 1908, Coors had begun to diversify his company into other industries, including real estate, cement, cooking china and porcelain. During Prohibition, he also would convert the brewery plant into a producer of malted milk and related products. In short, he was not finished.

Coors would spend the rest of his days and much of his money keeping alive Adolph Coors Brewing and Manufacturing Company, the name given his enterprises upon their incorporation in 1913, two years after Golden paved its streets and he bought his first automobile, a Stevens-Duryea. He already had named his eldest son, Adolph Jr., a partner in 1909 and superintendent of the brewery in 1912, and would rely more and more on Adolph Jr. and his other sons, Grover and Herman, to oversee operations — "his three greatest assets," Bill Coors says.

On gray winter days in the last years of his life, wearing a fur cap and overcoat, "Papa" Coors, as the employees called Adolph now, often strolled down to the lake he built on brewery grounds in 1902 and watched the ice-cutting and skaters. On a sunny day, however, he'd leave the fur cap home and wear his straw hat, prompting the employees to whisper, "Ah ha, Papa wants nice weather now to sell beer." Adolph was a born optimist.

The life of Adolph Coors has a sad epitaph. In 1929, he either fell or jumped to his death from the sixth-floor balcony of the Cavalier Hotel in Virginia Beach, Virginia, where he had gone to recuperate from the flu. Only he knows the facts of his death. "He was in poor health and overwhelmed by responsibility to his family and a struggling business," Bill Coors says. "Personally, I believe it all got to be too much."

It is a bitter irony that national Prohibition

Theo. Koch - 1910

was repealed fewer than four years after Adolph's death. Yet, his was a life of clear, purposeful and, above all, realized ambition. His adopted land indeed was the land of opportunity for him — Adolph Coors had become what he wanted to become. His legacy is the endurance of the company still bearing his name and the traditions of discipline and tenacity he set for succeeding generations.

"I can still see him standing on the front porch of his home in the early morning as an old, white-haired man," Bill Coors says. "He was frail and he walked slowly, but there he was in his pajamas and slippers exercising with a pair of cast iron dumbbells. We are not going to let that gentleman down."

This early Coors delivery truck hit the road in the 1910s. By that time, even Coors Golden Beer, below, had begun to feel the impact of the growing movement to ban alcoholic beverages. Though Coors had already begun to diversify into other businesses, the coming years would test the company's adaptability and determination.

The brewery's on-site "hospitality bar," tended by longtime bartender Alphonse Thuet, was open to brewery workers, as well as the public, with a per-person limit of two 12-ounce mugs. Thuet — fourth from the right in this 1894 picture — was a local legend, tending the bar before and after Prohibition. He served customers at his whim — an extra mug for a beautiful woman or none at all for people he felt were not welcome.

CHAPTER TWO

CAST

ANEW

A dolph Coors, Jr., was in many ways his father's duplicate. Like the older Coors, Adolph Jr. was pushed by hard work, an indefatigable drive and a never-say-die optimism. He was only 24 years old when he became his father's partner in 1909, seven years before the sale of alcohol became illegal in Colorado. During the lean Prohibition years, he assumed greater responsibility for running the family's enterprises, and after the death of Adolph Coors, adroitly guided the company's triumphant return to the beer business.

At home, however, Adolph Jr. was emotionally remote and distant — an inflexible, no-nonsense parent caught up entirely in his work. "My father wasn't happy unless he was working, and there was an awful lot of work to be done," Bill Coors reveals. "He just loved his family the only way he knew."

"He believed if he showed affection, it would spoil me and my brothers. There was no levity in the house, no idle chatter at the dinner table. If you didn't have something worth saying, my father felt you shouldn't say it. So if you had a little humorous tidbit you thought the family might enjoy, you'd sit there and weigh it over and, ultimately, just keep it to yourself.

Coors' laboratory for quality monitoring and the development of new beers was and is considered among the most technologically advanced in the world. On most days, Adolph Coors, Jr., a chemical engineer by trade, could be found working alongside the company's scientists. The new beers that emerged from Coors' laboratory, including Golden Select, below, fueled the company's growth in the first part of the twentieth century.

"The work force was his extended family; employees loved him, and he knew them all on a first-name basis. As his son, though, I never got a word of approval, nor did my brothers. Never a pat on the back or anything to build up self-esteem. A perfect job was expected of you; anything else was underperformance.

"I remember my first work assignment out of college in June. He sent me over to the porcelain plant with instructions to raise the yields, which were down 50 percent. He said, 'Do something about these losses,' adding, 'but don't change anything.'

"If you disagreed with him on any subject, he'd say, 'If you spent as much time thinking about this as I have, you'd come to the same conclusion.' Even when he was wrong, he could never admit it. I'd have to wait until he went out of town to change things.

"Still, he did extraordinary things for this company. From my grandfather he inherited a high standard of ethics, a basic philosophy of hard work to meet goals and considerable business acumen. These helped him build a world-class chemical porcelain company out of a failing pottery and reopen the brewery when hundreds of other family-owned breweries stayed closed.

"And, perhaps, most importantly, he raised and guided three sons to take this company even further."

Before Prohibition hit Colorado in 1916, the Golden Brewery basked in the sunshine of success. Sales climbed steadily, thanks in part to new beers like Golden Select. Technology provided new and better means of producing beer, and the brewery was continually renovated to incorporate more modern machinery.

New enterprises sprang up as well. In 1908, Adolph Coors, Sr., bought a stake in the failing United States Portland Cement Company. Coors' investment was influenced by personal as well as business reasons. His youngest daughter, Bertha, had married a dashing young mining engineer by the name of Harold S. Munroe. "My grandfather wanted to provide a job for his new son-in-law so his daughter could live nearby," Bill Coors recalls.

"Harold Munroe, a graduate of the Colorado School of Mines, operated the cement plant with great success against the Ideal Cement Co., owned by Charles Boettcher. 'Uncle Jack' Munroe had the wanderlust and soon tired of the cement business, which my grandfather then sold to Boettcher."

The elder Adolph also diversified into the pottery business. In 1910, at a Denver exhibition of pottery, he observed various pieces made from local clay by a potter named John J. Herold, who had come to Colorado to relieve his tuberculosis. Impressed by the quality of the work, Adolph Sr. offered Herold part of the old glass works to use as his studio — free of charge.

In December 1910, Herold incorporated the Herold China and Pottery Company. The fledgling enterprise manufactured tea sets, creamers, sugar bowls, heat-resistant cookware and spark plugs for automobiles and motorcycles.

Herold's health began to deteriorate, however, and in 1912, he abandoned the pottery and left Golden. To keep it alive, Adolph Coors and other Goldenites bought stock in the company. The new owners earmarked funds to build a second story on

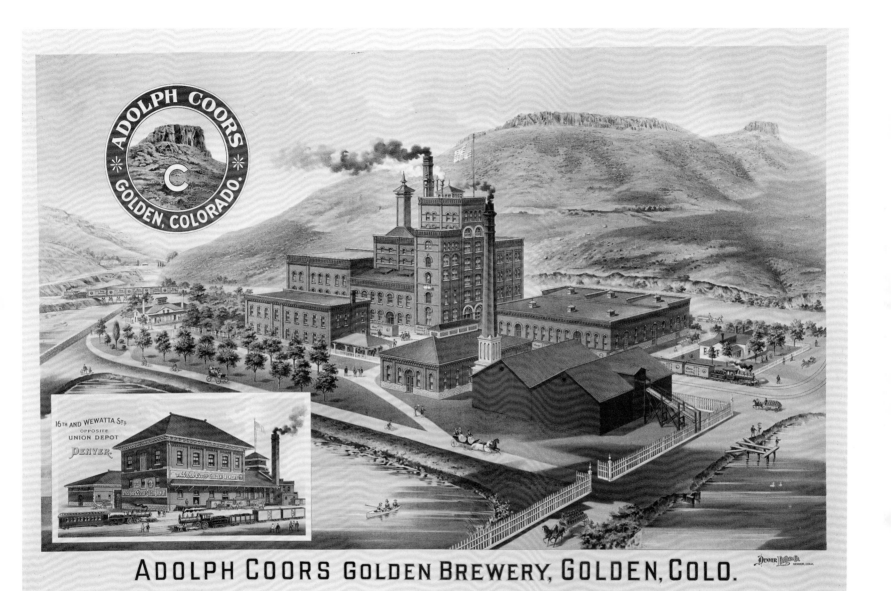

ADOLPH COORS GOLDEN BREWERY, GOLDEN, COLO.

the old glass works and buy a new kiln. Adolph invested between $8,000 and $10,000 in the venture and, in 1913, was elected president of the company. His oldest son, Adolph Jr., was elected vice president and manager.

In June 1913, Adolph Sr. restructured the company, changing it from a wholly owned proprietorship into a corporation in which he shared ownership with his three sons and three daughters. Since he had set aside substantial dowries for his daughters, Coors gave more shares to his sons.

With Adolph Jr. managing the pottery, Coors turned his attention to modernizing the brewery. He purchased a machine that produced ice at the "amazing rate of one ton per hour" and installed state-of-the-art, glass-lined storage tanks at the bottling plant. Coors also replaced the brewery's horse-drawn wagons with canvas-topped trucks.

This meticulously drafted lithograph illustrates the company's attention to landscaping and cleanliness. Adolph Coors desired a pleasant atmosphere for employees and visitors. The brewery was "as clean as the parlour of your home," a local newspaper reported.

Coors Porcelain Company manufactured inexpensive dinnerware, including the Rosebud Cook-N-Serve line featured to the left. The kiln above fired the pieces, which were decorated with an embossed hand-painted rose and leaf pattern. Adolph Coors established the pottery after viewing pieces created with Golden clay by a Midwestern potter named John J. Herold.

The pottery drew upon the abundance of natural clay found in Golden. Workers prepared the molds on the second story of Coors' old glass works. The *Colorado Transcript* reported that Coors was "building up a pottery business which bids fair to be one of the greatest institutions of its kind."

Caught in the Crossfire

Shortly before the outbreak of World War I, Adolph and Louisa Coors returned to Germany to visit the graves of Adolph's parents. It was their second trip to Germany and their first "round-the-world" tour.

Midway through the trip in the spring of 1914, however, the heir to the Austrian throne, Archduke Francis Ferdinand, was assassinated and Europe went to war. The couple was trapped on a continent in the thick of battle. Moreover, their touring automobile, a Pierce-Arrow, was confiscated by the French government. It would be several months before they could leave Europe — sans car.

Upon their return, life was not any easier. Golden's citizens, many of whom were of English descent, were alarmed by the Coors heritage. Even though they were naturalized citizens of the U.S.A., the Coors were the subjects of unjust suspicion and prejudice. They fought this malice with good deeds.

When the United States entered the war in 1917, Adolph and Louisa headed a list of contributors from Golden to the army's YMCA fund and the Liberty Loan campaign. Adolph forbade employees from speaking German at the plant, which until then had been the dominant language. Even the maids and cooks at the Coors residence had regularly spoken German. But not one German word was uttered again after Adolph's decree.

*T*all, lanky and soft-spoken, Adolph Coors, Jr., always was meticulously groomed and dressed. However, he was not above the grittier aspects of running a pottery. A trained chemical engineer, he spent countless hours experimenting with methods of producing chemical porcelain.

The year 1910 marked the brewery's best sales prior to Prohibition — 100,000 barrels — just a few thousand shy of that produced by Zang's Brewery, Colorado's largest. Coors' sales would decline precipitously thereafter, as city after city in the state went dry and "Sunday Laws" were enacted.

TENSIONS MOUNT AS WAR FEARS RISE

Travel figured prominently in the family's plans. For nearly three years, from 1909 to 1911, Adolph Jr. studied brewery methods in Vienna and Munich. Upon his return, he was a changed man — more European in manner and dress. He even developed the European custom of tipping his hat when meeting people.

Adolph and Louisa frequently traveled throughout the United States and in 1903 made their first trip abroad to Germany. In March 1914, the couple departed for a five-month, round-the-world tour. Midway through the trip, however, the heir to the Austrian throne, Archduke Francis Ferdinand, was assassinated in Sarajevo. Europe was soon at war.

Back in Golden, Adolph launched himself into the war effort on behalf of his native country, selling German war bonds to raise revenue for the Kaiser's battles against England. His efforts did not endear him to many Goldenites, however. The bulk of the city's population originated from Cornwall, England. "Though my grandfather had for many years been an American citizen, much slander was directed at him," Bill Coors says. "But he could not turn his back on his homeland — until certain events forced him to."

The sinking of the British passenger ship *Lusitania* by a German submarine in May 1915 aroused a wave of indignation in the United States. On board were 128 U.S. citizens — all of them lost their lives. Continuing German submarine warfare greatly influenced President Woodrow Wilson to declare war on Germany in 1917.

Immediately following the announcement, Adolph Coors switched his allegiance from Germany to the United States. He did so with a vengeance, heading a list of Golden contributors to both the Army YMCA fund and the Liberty Loan campaign. So furious was he over the attack that he forbade employees from ever again speaking German at the plant.

During the war, Coors also was instrumental in developing a much-needed product, chemical porcelain, a high-quality material used to contain various chemicals and dyes in scientific laboratory experiments. An embargo on German goods entering the United States cut off the entire supply of chemical porcelain, prompting the U.S. Department of Commerce to request U.S. potteries to fill the void.

Adolph Jr. and his younger brother, Herman Coors, were given the task of manufacturing the chemical ware — not an easy assignment. Laboratory porcelain must resist thermal shock, acids and alkalis and must also withstand extremely high temperatures. Fortunately, Adolph Jr.'s keen, analytical mind and his training as a chemical engineer put him in good stead to meet the task.

"Clad in flannel shirt and rough outer garb, and with his hands white with clay dust, Adolph Coors, Jr., is working with an energy which dispels the illusion that the sons of rich men have no real liking for hard work," the *Transcript* observed in February 1915. "He is at the factory at the opening hour in the morning and works all day, [this] expert chemist and ceramicist."

Despite setbacks, in 1915, COORS U.S.A. chemical porcelain made its debut. Adolph Jr. and Herman traveled to universities, chemical society meetings and trade shows to promote the product, and by 1916, the company's factory output fulfilled the needs of the entire United States.

Employment at the pottery jumped from 37 workers in 1915 to 75 in 1917. That year the name of the pottery was changed to Coors Porcelain Company.

In 1916, Herman Coors was named manager of the porcelain plant. A volunteer wrestling coach at the Colorado School of Mines, Herman was robust, headstrong and not a little impetuous. "When the traveling carnival came to town, Uncle Herman used to win five dollars taking up the challenge to toss the masked grappler out of the ring," Bill Coors quips. "But then he'd follow the carnival all around the area until they had to pay him to stay away."

NEAREST OF THEM ALL

Another brother, Grover Coors, would undertake another new enterprise — the brewing of malted milk and non-fermented cereal beverages. The first cereal beverage, called Mannah, was developed in August 1914 for sale to dry Colorado towns. Adolph Coors, Sr., his life spent as a brewer, is said to have tasted Mannah and remarked, "It looks like beer, and it smells like beer, but it tastes like…." Always the gentleman, he did not say the last word.

Nonetheless, the company's advertising overlooked the founder's distaste: "Coors Pure Cereal Beverage. Fine for home use — and enjoyed by the whole family. Try a case today. See how genuinely good this unusual drink is."

Production of Mannah ceased in 1916, due to wartime restrictions on grain, and was resumed in 1919. In 1921, the company modified how it made the beverage. A still was installed to brew and ferment real beer, and the alcohol produced was distilled off.

Coors sold the alcohol under bond to pharmacists, laboratories and industrial users, and stored it in government-bonded warehouses on Coors property. A federal employee was required on-premise during

Mannah was Coors' brand name for the "near beer" manufactured during Prohibition. The output of Mannah was one-tenth the output of beer before Prohibition. Coors' other enterprises during prohibition included malted milk, an idea suggested by Grover Coors' wife, Willimaine, who was connected to the Horlick family, then America's largest producer of malted milk.

Pass the Dictionary, Please

U p until the entry of the United States in World War I, virtually everyone at the brewery spoke fluent German. In fact, German was the first language Grover Coors, son of the founder, learned to speak. However, Grover's grammar was not equal to his spoken German. When Adolph Coors learned that Grover was not doing well in his German studies at Cornell University, Adolph Coors came up with a singular strategy for improving his son's German grammar skills.

"My grandfather required dear Uncle Grover to write all letters to him in German," says Bill Coors, thankful, it seems, he never met such reproof.

"Needless to say, Uncle Grover kept his letters as short as possible."

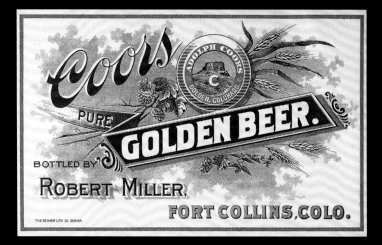

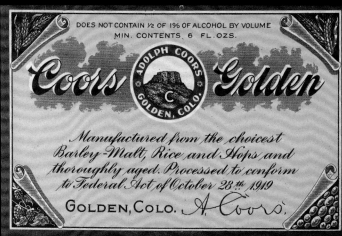

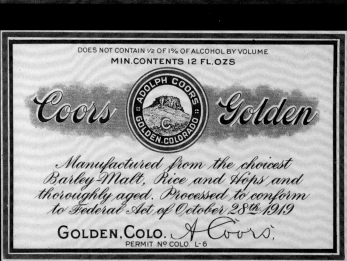

Coors' second line of near beer tasted much better than Mannah, thanks to a new brewing process. It was produced with the same method as real beer, and then the alcohol was distilled off. The company named this better-tasting near beer Coors Golden, building on the reputation established by its pre-Prohibition brew, Golden Beer, top

The Drink – that Delights Coors

PURE
CEREAL
BEVERAGE

working hours to make sure alcohol receipts and sales were properly documented and the appropriate tax, reportedly as high as $18 per gallon, was collected.

The 190-proof distillate served another, albeit illegal, purpose — as an intoxicating adjunct to many an anti-Prohibitionists' near beer. "There was a trick to this," Bill Coors chuckles. "You'd top off a bottle of near beer with alcohol, put your thumb on the open mouth and turn it upside down and then right side up. If the beer stayed in the bottle when you released your thumb, it was good near beer. Unfortunately, our near beer didn't fall into that category. The contents gushed forth like a small geyser."

Sales of Coors' new near beer, called Coors Golden, were but a fraction of its pre-Prohibition real beer volume, reaching a maximum of no more than 16,000 barrels a year. Bottling of the brew was done only two days a month in winter and 10 days a month in summer.

OF MILK AND HONEY

By 1917, the plight of the company as a result of Prohibition was apparent in the annual report, written in Adolph's handwriting and taking up all of one page. Revenues were $217,000; operating costs were $350,000. In short, the company was losing money.

Steps were taken to reduce expenses. Coors cut his salary from $15,000 per year to $10,000, and the salaries of his brother William and Adolph Jr., were reduced by $1,200 and $600, respectively. Of course, these measures were not enough to stop the fiscal bleeding. Revenues would have to increase sharply to keep the company alive.

Mannah was first known as a cereal beverage, but after the manufacturing process was improved, it tasted much more like real beer. After brewing the beverage, the alcohol was removed and sold under bond to chemists and pharmacists, below.

Offering some hope was the company's malted milk business, operated by Grover Coors. Since there were no textbooks on making malted milk, a dehydrated mixture of malt extract and whole milk, Grover learned through trial and error. He began experiments in 1914, buying special machinery and making mashes of ground-up malt and wheat. A year later, the *Transcript* reported Grover had "perfected" the process, producing 24 pounds of malted milk "equal in quality to the best made by any other factory." Indeed, moisture content in Coors malted milk was 10 percent less than any other brand due to Colorado's high altitude and low evaporation temperatures.

The old keg department at the brewery was retrofitted to accommodate the new venue. All brewing machinery was removed, and the walls, ceilings and floor were given a sanitary coating of white enamel. The company employed milk testers at $65 a month. Appeals for milk were widely circulated in the *Transcript*.

MILK
We Can Use Your Milk
The Year Round
Phone
A. Coors B&M Co. Golden 18

Within a few short months, arrangements were made with local farmers to deliver up to 2,500 gallons of milk each day at a price of 15 cents a gallon and up — depending on the butter fat content.

New machinery arrived in 1917, and a second work shift was added, keeping the plant operating day and night. Employees were on call at all times — even on Sundays — decked out in white gowns and caps to pack malted milk into cans or glue labels on jars.

Coors Malted Milk was deemed equal in quality to the best. "With their pure air, pure mountain water, perfect sanitary feeding and housing arrangements [for cows]," Coors has the "most ideal conditions for producing a perfect malted milk," the Colorado Transcript reported. The company's name during

Prohibition, Adolph Coors Brewing and Manufacturing Company, more accurately depicted the broad variety of products that kept the company afloat during those tough years. The card below touted several Prohibition-era products, namely Malted Milk, Flaked Milk Solids, Cereal Beverage and Malt Sugar.

Coors

PURE

MALTED MILK

A·DOLPH COORS
TRADE MARK
C
GOLDEN, COLORADO

SELECT BRAND

VERY HEALTHFUL AND NOURISHING

NEXT TO MOTHER'S MILK THE BEST FOOD FOR INFANTS
UNEQUALED FOR HOSPITAL AND FAMILY USE

**ACCEPTED BY
LEADING PHYSICIANS AND DRUGGISTS
AS SUPERIOR TO OTHER MALTED MILKS**

Adolph Coors kept Goldenites employed despite Prohibition. Brewery workers who had shoveled barley malt now produced malted milk candy tablets. Leonard Vogel, seated on the left, worked at Coors for more than 50 years — through many industry changes.

The product was sold in five-pound, ten-pound and twenty-five-pound tins. Malted milk tablets were marketed for candy store sales, as was an unsuccessful chocolate-flavored product called Troffe. The company also developed a small trade in related products, such as double cream, sweet cream butter, malt syrup, malt sugar, buttermilk and dried skim milk — called Coors Crystals.

Selling the merchandise was a force of salesmen, including three demonstration teams that appeared at food shows and drug stores. Coors also retailed malted milk to soda fountains and ice cream parlors. Ironically, some of them previously were saloons and taverns selling Coors Golden Lager.

The business was never much better than a break-even proposition. Competition was keen and revenues barely covered expenses. Setbacks dogged the company. In 1917, for example, an overenthusiastic salesman ordered several carlots of malted milk to be sold in larger cities. Most came back unsold.

Just when business looked its bleakest, help arrived. The Mars Candy Company, the well-known manufacturer of Milky Way, Snickers and other candy bars, was looking for a more competitively priced and higher quality source of malted milk and was interested in Coors' product.

After several meetings, Mars named Coors its main supplier of malted milk in 1925. With fully 95 percent of Coors' production sold to Mars, the malted milk storage room was empty most of the time. Product often went fresh from the dryer right into waiting railcars.

Although the plant's production was high, profits remained elusive. "Whenever my father traveled to Chicago to seek price relief to compensate our rising costs, he was told to forget it, that Mr. Mars would just build his own malted milk plant," Bill Coors says. "Somehow we met their price and stayed alive — barely."

For many Goldenites, the continuance of the malted milk plant and pottery was critical. Flu epidemics in 1917 and 1918 ravaged the small city, and some families lost two or more members to the disease. With men away at war, family finances were tightened and many children were sent to work. A 13-year-old girl working at Coors Porcelain in 1917 earned $4.32 a week for 48 hours work, paid in cash. It wasn't much, but it helped pay the bills.

ARMISTICE AT LAST

When the war ended in November 1918, the Golden fire bell awakened the town. An impromptu parade was quickly assembled and a bonfire was set on Washington Street in the heart of town. Louisa

Coors raised an American flag at a patriotic service held at the Army camp in Golden's city park, where bands played and many wept in joy.

The country stormed into the Roaring Twenties, a period of profound cultural enhancement, economic prosperity and unbridled personal liberty. Unemployment plunged from 12 percent to 3.2 percent between 1920 and 1929, and everybody, it seemed, had cash to burn.

The 1920s were one long party, indeed. Audacious flappers in shockingly short hairstyles balanced martini glasses while dancing the Charleston, their long strands of pearls swinging seductively. Bathtubs overflowed with bootleg gin, and speakeasies replaced boarded-up taverns and bars.

Although alcohol was illegal, it was not unobtainable. Quality, however, was another matter. "Some bootleggers are poor businessmen," the *Transcript* wrote in 1925. "They're killing off people so fast with poison booze that they will soon run out of customers!"

That was not likely.

Coors employees made the best of the decade — even without real beer. On weekend nights, many workers frequented the Castle Rock Dance Hall, built in 1919, on the top of Castle Rock. Revelers were ferried up and down the mountain by cable cars strung along its side. On Sunday afternoons, employees cheered the company football team, the Potters, at Golden's Brooks Field. Others participated on the company bowling and basketball teams.

Pay in the 1920s was $1.50 a day for an eight-hour workday, paid twice a month in cash in a small envelope. After they pocketed the money, employees were asked to return the envelope for reuse. Adolph Jr. was ever frugal.

Hiring procedures were not particularly rigorous — for some. One retiree recalled that in 1921, he went to the bottle house and "just started working. After I'd been working two or three days, the foreman said, 'Hey, kid, are you working here?' and I said, 'Yeah, I'm working here.'" The new employee's name was put on a timecard.

Many workers were jockeyed from one Coors enterprise to another. When bottling of Coors Golden was in high gear, employees in other departments were sent over to pitch in. When not bottling, employees did construction or maintenance work. Never idle, some even made cleaning brushes from hog bristle and wire.

At home, the Coors adults grappled with the antics of the next generation — Adolph Jr.'s sons, Adolph III (nicknamed "Ad"), Bill and Joe. The boys had the run of the brewery grounds and made good use of the privilege, cooking up whatever mischief they could. "The temptation to horse around was irresistible," Bill Coors acknowledges. "We were pretty close to being juvenile delinquents, heckling the hell out of the workers and stealing tidbits out of their lunch baskets and all."

Unable to discipline the boys after each offense, Adolph Jr. developed a novel method of punishment. On Sundays, his only day of rest, he meted out corrections for the entire previous week. "Our mother kept an accurate log of our misdeeds, and we were made to suffer appropriately for each one," Bill Coors confesses. "We'd emerge from the ordeal with our sins atoned and our guilt purged, already plotting the next week's mischief."

Sundays are remembered less-than-fondly for another reason. It was the boys' haircut day — a half-inch long in winter and "pretty much bald" in summer.

FAMILY TIES AND TIFFS

Adolph Jr., however, had more serious family troubles than his sons' pranks. Herman Coors disagreed repeatedly with him and their father over the direction of the porcelain company. Herman offered to buy the company, and when that offer was refused, he left Golden in the mid-1920s and launched a

The second generation of Coors children pose for a portrait with their mother, Louisa Coors, seated. From left to right are Bertha Munroe, Louise Porter, Adolph Coors, Jr., Grover Coors, Herman Coors and Augusta Colbran.

Hollywood High Life

In 1924, Grover Coors, the son of the company's founder, headed west to California, where he eventually became the company's beer representative. Grover was the much-loved "black sheep" of the family, a hard-drinking free spirit who loved beer, women and song.

Everett Barnhardt, a Coors retiree who spent a fair share of time with Grover during his "Hollywood years" (as Barnhardt calls them), recalled that Grover often conducted business in the "Passion Pit," a lounge in the Hollywood Roosevelt Hotel that was his favorite haunt. "Grover held forth in the Passion Pit nearly every night," Barnhardt wrote. "Many Hollywood actors and actresses visited the Pit and [they] all knew Grover."

As for Coors' beer sales in California, the company's largest state market at the time, Barnhardt noted that "small amounts were sent to various distributors in the Bay area and to W.C. Fields in Hollywood, [but] most of the beer sent to California was consumed by Grover and his personal friends."

W.C. Fields was among those Grover Coors counted as friends in his heyday in Hollywood. "Bill" Fields noted on this photo for Grover that he was not just a friend but a fan of Coors beer.

competing porcelain company in Englewood, California. The business eventually was turned over to his sons.

Grover Coors also had a falling out with Adolph Jr. The younger Coors married into a fast crowd, a group of wealthy, second-generation Coloradans who played hard and drank hard — despite Prohibition. After divorcing his first wife, Willimaine, Grover remarried into the jet set, much to his family's chagrin. "This lovely man started spending money like there was no tomorrow," Bill Coors recalls. "He was dedicated to the party circuit, something the hardworking males in the family had neither the time nor money for." In 1924, Grover also headed west to California, where he eventually became the company's beer representative.

Following the departure of his brothers, and the death of Adolph Coors, Sr., in 1929, Adolph Jr. became the guiding force of the company. He threw all his energy into building the business. It was a challenge that would require that and more.

UPS AND DOWNS AND UPS

In 1926, Germany re-entered the chemical porcelain market with products costing 50 percent less than the price charged by Coors and other leading manufacturers. Despite intense capital pressures caused by a recent large addition to the porcelain plant, Coors was forced to match the price.

Problems confronted the malted milk facility as well. The malt dryer broke down in 1929, and there was a significant delay in receiving a new one. Fortunately, there was enough malted milk in storage to meet existing orders. New orders, however, had to wait.

As a whole, the malted milk, near beer, pottery and porcelain enterprises were unprofitable, and the company barely kept afloat. Once again, serendipity intervened. While the stock market crash of 1929 had little effect on Coors, the financial turmoil it produced fueled a movement to repeal Prohibition to generate new jobs.

Adolph Jr. and other former brewers met in Chicago in 1933 to discuss the framework for repeal. They agreed the end of Prohibition would come only when the president of the United States backed such a position. The brewers threw their weight behind New York Governor Franklin Delano Roosevelt and his promise of a "New Deal."

FDR's opponent in the election was President Herbert Hoover, an ardent Prohibitionist and lifelong teetotaler. Roosevelt won in a landslide, and on March 22, 1933, he signed a bill permitting the manufacture and sale of beer and wine. The following year, Congress enacted the 21st Amendment legalizing all alcoholic beverages.

Bill Coors was studying at Phillips Exeter Academy in New Hampshire when he learned the news. "I read in the paper — to my utter disbelief — that Prohibition had been repealed," he says. "I knew immediately the company had a new lease on life."

REBUILDING FROM THE BOTTOM UP

"Happy Days Are Here Again" screamed a huge banner hung over New York's Times Square the moment the sale of beer once again became legal. In Washington, throngs of people applauded a truck headed for the White House bearing a sign reading, "President Roosevelt, the first beer is for you." Nearly everyone cheered the return of beer.

Adolph Jr. had a decided advantage over other enterprising brewers looking to get back into business — the three years he spent in Munich and Vienna studying technical and practical brewing methods. "There were few people in this country in 1933 who were more capable of starting up a brewery than my father," Bill Coors says.

Indeed, of the 1,568 breweries in the country prior to Prohibition, only 750 reopened in 1933. The law required each of them to wait 15 days before selling their beer — an excruciating time for many. "The real beer...is ready now in the big vats," the *Transcript* placated. "It will be only the matter of seconds to bottle and cap the beverage [for] thirsty customers."

A parade of delivery trucks lined up to leave the brewery at 12 a.m., April 7, 1933, the end of the waiting period. "We worked all that night," recalled a former employee. "It was thrilling."

When the clock struck midnight, the Coors brewery was officially back in business. As they trundled out of town, rumor had it that some trucks were hijacked on the outskirts of Golden by overzealous beer drinkers.

Manufacturing capacity was set at 300 barrels a day, requiring more workers at the plant. Employment soon skyrocketed, from 67 in 1933

Above, the town of Golden welcomed the end of Prohibition with the brightly lit signs of taverns and the bustle of Coors' resurgent business. The large map spread across the exterior of the building at right points out the highlights of the Golden area to visitors entering downtown Golden.

THE ROCKY MOUNTAIN NEWS

Colorado's First Newspaper—Since 1859

VOLUME 74: NO. 97   DENVER, COLO., FRIDAY, APRIL 7, 1933   IN TWO SECTIONS—SECTION ONE

REVIVAL OF STATE INDUSTRY MARKS LEGAL BEER'S RETURN

Business Hums as Legal Beer Returns to State

Vast Sums of Cash Put in Circulation to Produce Brew

TRUCKS LOADED FOR NIGHT DASH

Stroke of 12 Signal for Cargo Race to Buyers' Doors

BY ROBERT L. CHASE

To the tune of humming machinery, clanging locomotives, banging hammers and jingling cash, legal beer has returned to Colorado.

Brewers, distributors, licensing authorities and workers in scores of industries went at top speed all day yesterday so that the flow of 3.2 per cent beer might start on its way to consumers at Thursday midnight.

The big rush was in the licensing

A*fter Prohibition was repealed, Coors began to expand outside Colorado. Coors draught beer was packaged in oak barrels, which were transported by rail or truck to wholesalers and distributors in the West. Customers outside Colorado sometimes needed some persuasion to try Coors, but soon customers clamored for Coors beer "brewed in Golden, Colorado."*

to 199 in 1934. The brewery buzzed with people scurrying from one building to another — there were eight in all by 1936. Among the workers was Alphonse Thuet, who returned to his old job dispensing hospitality and beer as the brewery's onsite bar attendant, an occupation he began in 1889.

Hourly pay increased from roughly 40 cents an hour before Prohibition to about 60 cents an hour afterwards — the highest rate of pay in the brewery industry. Even inexperienced, new help received 56 and a quarter cents per hour.

The workers joined Local #366, representing the brewery union in Colorado. The union had been on strike during Prohibition, and after a 20-year absence, Adolph Jr. personally invited it back. Thus began almost 20 years of peaceful relations between Coors and the labor union.

On April 13, 1933, Coors' first beer ad in 17 years appeared in the *Transcript*, placed there by the Chocolate Shop, the first establishment in Golden to obtain a beer license. It read: Golden's Own Coors' GOLDEN BEER Note Its Beautiful Amber Color. The price was $3.60 a case, "Cooled If Ordered." Two weeks later, the newspaper reported the demand for pretzels had more than doubled since the return of real beer.

The 21st Amendment outlawed tied houses — the saloons and other beer distributing enterprises previously owned by Coors and other breweries. Taverns and distributors had to be privately owned, and Coors went about courting and signing up independent distributors.

In Colorado, the company appointed two distributors in 1933, increasing to six within a couple years. It also appointed a distributor in Arizona. Four years later, Southern California was added to the distribution area and headed up by Grover Coors. Distributors in New Mexico, Nevada, Wyoming, Kansas and Oklahoma were appointed in 1938, and in Idaho and Utah the following year.

Altogether, Coors products were distributed by a wide variety of businesses, including soft drink bottlers and tobacco, grocery and liquor wholesalers. Some distributors drove to the brewery in their own trucks to pick up beer, while others had it shipped to them by rail.

In 1934, the company bought 40 freight cars and painted them white with gold lettering proclaiming "Coors Golden." Affixed to each car was the Castle Rock illustration with a large "C" just below the castle.

Territorial sales representatives were assigned to specific distributors and states to market Coors beer. They traveled by train or truck to visit distributors and retail accounts, helping them stock and rotate the product and place point-of-sale advertisements. A few even grabbed a paintbrush to paint "Coors" on warehouse walls. Thus began a long and mutually profitable relationship between Coors and its distributors.

Outside Colorado, it sometimes required ingenuity to get consumers to try a bottle of Coors. "I used to take a cooler of beer along on the truck when I was traveling, and if I saw a tractor out in the field, I would wave the guy over for a cold Coors," one sales representative recalled. "Then I would say, 'Now when you go to town, remember how good this cold Coors tastes.'"

In 1933, the company sold 90,350 barrels of beer — 70 percent draught — about what it expected. Several years and much adversity would pass, however, before sales increased appreciably. Industry laws needed to be clarified and amended, buildings

needed to be renovated and sales and marketing systems needed to be established. Slowly and surely these began to fall into place.

BUILDING A BREWERY FOR THE FUTURE

Like his father, Adolph Jr. was committed to making the highest quality beer possible. "If you wanted to find him, he was never in his office — he was always in the laboratory," Bill Coors remembers.

"He was constantly experimenting, constantly working, driving to make beer as good as it could be made. He figured the better the beer, the easier it would be to sell."

To improve the caliber of Coors beer, the company experimented with different strains of barley. In 1936, Ray Frost, Coors' office manager, received a small sample of "Moravian" barley from a malt supplier in Czechoslovakia. Frost took the seeds home and planted them. That fall he showed about 20 plants to Coors' top brass, who were so impressed they encouraged further genetic development. Ultimately, Moravian barley became a brewery staple.

Coors added a new beer in 1937, based on Adolph Jr.'s analysis that younger palates were turning to lighter beers. The new Pilsner-style beer, later named "Banquet," was lighter in both color and body than Coors' other brand at the time, Export Lager. The company adopted two slogans to adver-

BARLEY DAYS

"Barley is to beer as grapes are to wine," Bill Coors is fond of saying. As a brewery that has always placed quality above all other considerations in the brewing of beer, Coors' barley would have to be something special. It is.

In the company's earliest days, local farmers were contracted to grow barley that was malted right at the brewery, unlike other breweries that had outside suppliers malt barley for them. Coors remains the only major brewer that malts all its own barley.

Barley is the most important solid ingredient in beer and a major factor in its quality and taste. Coors beer was so esteemed that newspapers touted its salubrious properties. "Physicians recommend the use of Coors beer to patients needing a mild, healthful pure tonic," the *Globe* reported in 1892.

In 1937, after receiving a few barley seeds from a supplier in Moravia, Czechoslovakia, Coors switched to a new strain of barley it dubbed "Moravian." Since then, the company's geneticists at its barley gene bank in Burley, Idaho, have continually refined the strain to improve plant characteristics and the taste of Coors beer.

Each year, Coors celebrates the importance of barley with five festivals in major growing areas — Barley Field Days — honoring its more than 1,000 barley growers in Colorado, Wyoming, Idaho and Montana. At the 1997 Barley Field Day held at Fickel Park in Berthoud, Colorado, several hardworking farmers and their spouses held back tears as they received awards for crop quality, environmental stewardship and lifetime achievement. "The relationship we have with our growers is very special," Bill Coors says. "This kind of emotional connection is not something you see every day in business."

Coors uses top-quality barley grown by regional farmers in Colorado, Wyoming, Montana and Idaho. These fields are full of Coors' special two-row barley, a company staple.

tise the new beer: "Brewed with Pure Rocky Mountain Spring Water" and "America's Fine Light Beer."

Coors introduced another, even lighter beer in 1941 — the first Coors Light. Available in dark, stubby bottles and cans, it advertised "13 percent

The first Coors Light was advertised as a lower calorie beer. Although discontinued during World War II, a new recipe would return 30 years later to become the fourth largest-selling beer in the country.

calories less due to less solids." The beer was discontinued during World War II due to material shortages, although a highly successful version of it would return a generation later.

Adolph Jr.'s quality initiatives were abetted by more modern equipment. A new brewing unit, mash and brew kettles and a mash filter were installed in 1935, and a new aging cellar was constructed. The first one-piece, glass-lined beer storage tanks in the industry were introduced in 1934, and a tin can line filling an "astonishing" 150 cans per minute was unveiled in 1936. Tin cans weighed less than bottles, required no deposit and did not allow the contents to be subjected to light.

WORKING AND PLAYING TOGETHER

Working at Coors in the late 1930s to the early 1940s was a happy time. "A family atmosphere prevailed," wrote one former employee. "The plant executives from Mr. Coors on down mingled with the crowd, swapped yarns, patted backs, wished one another well and had a grand and glorious time."

During the Christmas holidays, employees displayed their vocal and instrumental talents at the annual Christmas party in the auditorium. Mr. and Mrs. Adolph Coors, Jr., usually attended the parties, bringing eggnog in immense porcelain bowls for all to partake.

Thar She Blows

Adolph Coors, Jr., was known for his daily walks around the plant. Dressed impeccably, down to his goatskin shoes, he liked to visit with employees in the brewery and bottling house and taste the beer. On these excursions, he would tidy up the plant along the way, picking up and discarding cigarette butts left outside buildings.

One day, he was walking through the wort cooling area and saw an open tank door. Just as he peered into the tank, a worker was hoisting his hose to clean it, unaware the company's president was nearby. Adolph Jr. was soaked.

The worker was sure he was about to be fired, but Adolph, Jr., said it was his own fault for sticking his nose where it shouldn't have been. He turned, politely tipping his hat, and walked away, the goatskin shoes squish, squishing as he went.

Another popular company affair was the annual "Buckskin Party." Five or six Coors hunters would bring back 10 to 12 deer and other game from their exploits, which was aged at the ice plant and cooked and served during the holidays.

Many Coors employees traveled to work on the two inter-urban streetcars linking Denver and Golden, Nos. 83 and 84. Those who took No. 83 didn't have far to walk to work once in Golden — the streetcar stopped directly across the street from the company's office on 32nd Avenue.

No. 83 also had a clear view of the Coors' residence and its immense, beautiful lawn, upon which the words "Coors Malted Milk" were outlined in flowers. As the company grew, however, it became necessary to move the residence east of the present brewery, and the lawn and flowers were significantly reduced.

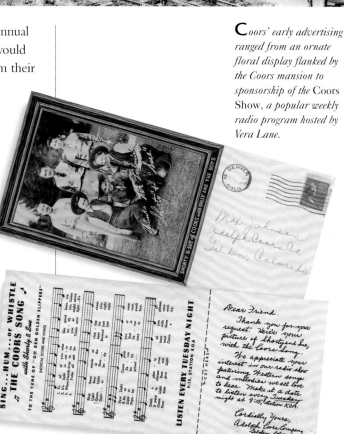

Coors' early advertising ranged from an ornate floral display flanked by the Coors mansion to sponsorship of the Coors Show, *a popular weekly radio program hosted by Vera Lane.*

Coors sponsored several semiprofessional sports teams during the period, including an all-African American baseball team, "one of the best," the *Transcript* reported. Such pros as Vic Raschi of the New York Yankees got their start on a Coors team.

The company also sponsored the *Coors Show*, a variety-style radio program featuring top performers and celebrities such as Duke Ellington and Mel Torme. The half-hour entertainment first aired in

The Coors Show *was a top Colorado radio program in the 1940s which featured many popular entertainers of the day and music ranging from the phenomenal band of* Duke Ellington, to the "nation's leading western entertainers," Shorty and Sue. The live broadcasts brought people to downtown Denver to witness the show.

Souvenir Folder of the
Coors Show

starring
Shorty, Sue, Sally and the Boys

The Nation's Leading Western Entertainers . . . Originators of "Saddle Rockin' Rhythm"

An "army" of Coors truck drivers delivered bottled beer and kegs to a nine-state region in the mid-1940s, their trucks emblazoned with "Coors — Brewed with Pure Rocky Mountain Spring Water." During the war, Coors advertised for engineers to help in its war-related chemical porcelain production efforts. The company eventually developed the insulators used in the U.S. atomic weapons program.

1942, on Thursday nights at 7:30. Vera Lane was the mistress of ceremonies and music was provided by Lloyd Wilkinson and The 25 Gentlemen of Note.

In 1940, the company reported 325 employees, most of whom had never worked in a brewery and needed training. This was quite a job, as the exactness and cleanliness required by Adolph Jr. was something many men had never known or seen before.

Smoking was forbidden, forcing employees to smoke in clusters outside — much like today. During his daily promenade around the plant, Adolph Jr. was known to pick up and discard the cigarette butts he saw along the way.

Adolph Jr. spoke to every employee he encountered. He had been a brewery worker just like them in the early part of the century, and they never forgot it. Indeed, the brewery union at Coors refused to work in 1907 unless Adolph Jr. was appointed their foreman, a position he held for a short while.

Adolph Jr. treated employees as collaborators. He never gave direct orders, "transmitting his wishes and feelings as suggestions or questions," one former employee wrote. "And when he delegated a job to someone, he refused to interfere in the carrying out of that job, unless the person proved incapable."

The company's leader enjoyed fraternizing with his fellow workers. "On Saturday afternoons, he'd come down to the lunchroom and have a beer with us," another employee recalled. "He'd have this small cup with him, and after a first beer, I'd ask him if he wanted another. 'Just half,' he'd say, and he meant it. He always stressed economy."

There were many memorable employees during this period, including tobacco-chewing John Silverthorn, Coors' head bookkeeper; Ed Green, the company's secretary; and bow-tied, bespectacled Everett Barnhardt. Barnhardt started as an office boy in 1933, making $40 a month cleaning spittoons and running errands for Adolph Jr. He ended his career as a director and vice president of the company.

Adolph Coors, Jr., carried the entire weight of the company on his shoulders. He toiled six days a week, sometimes half the day Sunday, keeping Coors alive. He guided the company through the turbulent Prohibition era, despite many setbacks and unprofitable enterprises. When the production of beer became legal once again, his background studying brewing techniques in Europe positioned the company to make a successful return to the beer business.

A Refusal to Compromise

When the United States entered the war in Europe following the bombing of Pearl Harbor, breweries across the nation coped with shortages of ingredients. To meet market demand and keep sales flowing, many breweries watered down their beer. Not Coors.

Adolph Jr.'s refusal to compromise the quality of Coors beer kept production low and sales flat during the war. Overseas, however, G.I.s from Coors' 11-state marketing region spread word of the beer's taste and quality — what later became known as the "Coors Mystique." When the war ended, demand for Coors beer intensified and sales exploded.

Through it all, Adolph Jr. kept working — six days a week and between 10 and 16 hours a day. "He worked himself to the bone," Bill Coors says. "He was six feet tall, but he was as thin as a rail. He'd drop down to about 119 pounds, and my mother would send him to a sanitarium in Santa Barbara to put some weight back on. He'd come back 10 pounds heavier, and then he'd lose the weight in a matter of months."

Adolph Coors, Jr., worked at the company virtually until his death at the age of 86 in 1970. Driving his intense involvement over the decades was a deep, personal sense of corporate responsibility and stewardship. His dedication and devotion was extolled by *Fortune* magazine in 1952, which named him one of Colorado's top business leaders. He nurtured Coors from a virtually unknown company producing less than 100,000 barrels of beer in 1933 to a nationally recognized brewery producing more than 7 million barrels per year at the time of his death. During that interval, he maintained the loyalty of his employees, the respect of his competitors and the friendship of many business associates. "My father reinvented what his father had passed on to him and built it into something much larger," Bill Coors says.

"Now it was up to me and my brothers to preserve and improve what he had given to us. We were ready."

Detour

A few yards from the original site of the Coors mansion was an old ironwood tree. Adolph Coors liked nothing more than to sit under that tree in the glare of summer sunlight, smoke a cigar and drink a glass of wine. Close to the tree was the residence of Grover Coors, which later became the residence of Joe Coors, Sr. Pete Coors, Joe's son, recalls that as a boy, the tree was a formidable third base in the backyard baseball games he played with his brothers.

When Joe Coors' residence was being demolished in the 1960s to make room for the brewery's expansion, Adolph Coors, Jr., demanded that under no circumstances must the old ironwood be damaged or removed. "It was his personal desire that this tree be preserved," wrote Everett Barnhardt, a Coors retiree.

After the new brewery was built, Barnhardt noted that the tree stayed. "Many a truck driver hated this tree with a passion because of the problem it presented in the attempt to maneuver their vehicles around it," he wrote.

When the residence was moved to make room for the expanding brewery in 1964, the tree was transplanted to the new site. The tree still grows near the mansion, an ode to yesteryear.

A lone assembly line worker monitors bottles of Coors as they slip smoothly into boxes for delivery. When beer became legal again in 1933, pre-Prohibition wooden cases were pressed into service until cardboard cartons could be designed and manufactured. Initially, bottles were packed by hand, four at a time. Some packers recalled that their fingers had to be bandaged to protect them from the sharp-edged metal tops of the crowns.

CHAPTER THREE

CHARGE AHEAD

As a teenager, Bill Coors dreamed of being a surgeon, but his father, Adolph Coors, Jr., steered him instead toward a degree in chemical engineering. Prior to graduating from Princeton University in 1939, Bill signed up to work at DuPont — without informing his father. When his parents came east for the commencement, however, Adolph Jr. looked so drawn and tired Bill didn't have the heart to tell him. The next day, he called DuPont and said he had changed his mind. With nary a glance back, he hopped a train to Golden and began working for the family business.

"When I came to work full-time in 1939, I didn't have an official position as such," Bill recalls. "I applied myself wherever I thought I could help, sanding the rough spots even though I was pretty much of a greenhorn.

"A few years later — during the war — I'd graduated to running operations at the brewery and the porcelain company. I didn't serve in the armed forces because I was needed at the porcelain plant, which was considered essential to the war effort. My younger brother, Joe, also received a military exemption for work-related reasons, and our older brother, Ad, received one for physical reasons.

America's Fine Light Beer

Coors

Although other brewers would benefit by introducing lower calorie beers, Coors always prided itself as "America's Fine Light Beer." In later years, the company was compelled to introduce an even lighter beer to meet growing demand for low calorie brews. Coors Light took the marketplace by storm, becoming one of the most popular beers in the world.

"Ad was the only one of us not to have a chemical engineering degree, and I believe that hampered him. Sometimes he had to bite his tongue and go along with the will of the mass. Joe, on the other hand, was a clone of my father, set in his ways and almost as stubborn. He received his chemical engineering degree from Cornell in 1940, and — unlike me — went to work for DuPont. A few years later, he took a job at a milk products company back east.

"When our beer sales skyrocketed after the war, my father sent me to talk Joe into leaving his job and helping us out. Joe agreed and took over the porcelain company so I could focus my attention on the brewery. He did a great job, bringing it out of the Middle Ages and making it tops in its field.

"The three of us worked with our father as a team during the 1940s, 1950s and 1960s. Not that there was always agreement — four strong-willed people in one room guarantees conflict. Our father, however, would not tolerate dissension. If there was a difference of opinion, he insisted we sit there and argue things out until we reached unanimity. We were then bound by the decision. It is a testament to my father's strength of character that we held the line.

"I was always the family maverick, coming up with ideas my father and brothers at first thought were off the wall, like developing an aluminum beverage can or sterilizing the brewing process so we wouldn't have to pasteurize our beer. Looking back, though, these ideas separated Coors from other breweries, in terms of innovation and excellence.

"As the years passed, our sales climbed higher, reaching a zenith of sorts in the mid-1970s, when nearly everybody in America who couldn't get a Coors beer in their home state wondered just what was in those cans."

World War II was a time of material shortages for the nation and, by extension, the brewery at Adolph Coors Company. The beer industry was deemed "non-essential" by the U.S. government and had extreme difficulties obtaining both gasoline and tires, making deliveries difficult.

While Coors could do little about the gasoline shortage, it was able to address the scarcity of tires. The company struck an agreement with a local tire dealer to buy used and recapped truck tires. Even with the "new" tires, however, the brewery still was forced to cut back truck deliveries to only once a week.

During the war, Coors also coped with reduced availability of bottles, bottle caps, labels, tin cans and, perhaps most importantly, labor. On the bright side, the government did make special allowances to assure that Coors and other breweries could buy enough barley and other raw materials for continued production — so long as they aided the war effort by setting aside half their beer for sale to the military. While it may have been a nonessential industry, beer was viewed as important to the morale of U.S. troops.

The brewery's sales during the war were erratic, hovering around 150,000 barrels a year, give or take. Much of this production was draught beer sold to taverns, which had become more popular as gathering places for people to discuss recent events and the progress of the war.

Although sales at the brewery were sluggish, the porcelain plant was alive with activity. The

During World War II, other breweries coped with material shortages by adding water to their beers — not Coors. Adolph Coors, Jr., insisted Coors beer stick to strict quality specifications, even if it resulted in lower profits. It was a prescient decision. After the war, word of Coors taste and quality spread from coast to coast, thanks to the many servicemen and women who trained in Colorado.

insulators to the Y-12 uranium plant at Oak Ridge, Tennessee.

"When atomic scientists were ready to pull the switch at Oak Ridge and found the insulators defective, they called on Coors," *Fortune* magazine reported.

When the war ended on August 14, 1945, Americans danced in the streets. Returning vets came home to their waiting families, and their gals knitted them argyles. Benny Goodman, Duke Ellington and Artie Shaw became household names, and everybody danced to Chick Webb's "Stomping at the Savoy."

Coors' returning heroes were warmly welcomed back to the company. Many returned to their previous occupations, although a few with newly acquired skills were given different positions. When everyone was finally reactivated, a semblance of normalcy returned to the brewery.

No sooner did they fall into their usual routines than — kaboom!— beer sales ignited. "When the service men and women returned home after the war, they asked for, talked about and wished they could get their hands on our beer," Bill Coors enthuses.

"In most cases, they were unable to, since the beer was available in only a few states." Word spread, and the Coors name developed an enigmatic reputation. The media eventually latched onto the story and gave this passion for Coors beer a name — the Coors Mystique.

SELLING THE WORLD'S BEST BEER

As the nation reverted to a peacetime economy, price controls on most commodities ended, industrial production heightened and a new consumer culture with greater disposable income emerged. To manage the brewery's burgeoning sales, Adolph Jr. turned to his oldest son, Adolph Coors III — or "Ad" as he preferred to be called.

Ad assembled a group of top sales representatives

This single engine plane was Coors' primary transportation link to its wholesalers throughout its marketing region.

Adolph III, seen here, headed up Coors' advertising team during the 1950s.

government bought a wealth of ceramic housings for land mines, as well as large quantities of chemical porcelain for industrial laboratories at home and overseas. The plant also provided high temperature

MYSTIQUE MADNESS

Prior to its national expansion in the 1980s, Coors' limited distribution left consumers in the eastern United States clamoring for a taste of the Rocky Mountains' finest beer. Many went to great lengths to experience what became known as the "Coors Mystique."

President Gerald Ford, for example, was known to return from his "Western White House" in Colorado accompanied on Air Force One by several cases of Coors. Apparently, Ford's secretary of state, Henry Kissinger, also had a hankering for the brew. Rumors circulated that Kissinger's armored limousine once was flown from California to the capital filled with 40 cases of Coors!

Even Hollywood took notice: the Burt Reynolds movie, *Smokey and the Bandit*, detailed the mustachioed hero's exploits smuggling a truckload of Coors beer to

Atlanta. Many Eastern fraternities also made it a part of their initiation rituals for pledges to drive to Colorado and bring back the prized bounty, which they dubbed "Rocky Mountain Kool-Aid."

Although it did not regret the fantastic press such illegal trafficking brought it,

Coors did bemoan the fact that the beer often was sold at distressed quality and higher prices. Today, of course, anyone in the United States (and in much of the rest of the world) can get a cold Coors of optimum quality and taste in their local markets — legally. Even President Ford.

*A*ctor Burt Reynolds partakes of a Coors on a break from filming Smokey and the Bandit. *The highly successful movie chronicled Reynolds' exploits smuggling Coors beer outside its distribution area, underscoring the tremendous appeal of Coors.*

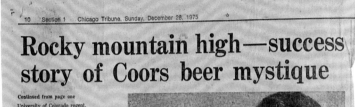

10   Section 1   Chicago Tribune, Sunday, December 28, 1975

Rocky mountain high—success story of Coors beer mystique

Continued from page one

University of Colorado regent.

This year, to the company's dismay, Coors has been in the headlines regularly, thanks to a Supreme Court ruling against its restrictive distribution policies; thanks, also, to the first public sale of some of its nonvoting stock; to Joseph Coors's CPB nomination, and to a lawsuit by the federal Equal Employment Opportunity Commission charging the company with race and sex discrimination.

In many ways Coors is the perfect product of the American free-enterprise system to which its top officials regularly pay homage. Since Adolph Coors began bottling the brew in 1873, the operatin has expanded into a $585-million business, employing about 7,500 persons, most of them in the brewery and related facilities sprawled on 31,000 acres in Golden. It has climbed from 12th in national sales in 1965 to fourth [behind Budweiser, Schlitz and Pabst], even though it is distributed in only 11 western states, while its competitors are selling throughout the country.

It is the leader in all but one of its states, the exception being Texas [where it is not distributed in all areas]. Moreover, it has captured the No. 4 spot with a bare minimum of paid advertising.

OVER THE YEARS the company has acquired its own barley fields, rice-milling facilities, construction crew, aluminum-can manufacturing plant, and trucks, so that it relies on the outside world for as little help as possible. Coors even owns some natural-gas reserves to supply its plants with fuel.

But it is not so much the product as the mystique surrounding it that is fascinating. It seems to have won a reputation as the elixir of beers, the brew of Presidents, a prize to be smuggled into the East the way Americans abroad used to smuggle in contraband copies of Henry Miller's novels.

Paul Newman, the king of beer-drinking actors, is said to require Coors on ice at all his movie sets. Henry Kissinger regularly brought cases back to Washington each time he made a trip to California.

Secret Service agents were forbidden to bring extra crates aboard federal planes after one agent was discovered to have loaded 38 cases onto a recent flight from the West Coast.

Holding a can of Coors, Paul Newman talks with his wife Joanne Woodward at a New York party.   AP Wirephoto

*I*n the 1970s, actor Paul Newman often was photographed toting his favorite brew in hand — a cold Coors. Here Newman sports a tux, goatee and a Coors alongside his wife, actress Joanne Woodward. The company didn't mind the free publicity one bit.

The Coors Brewery Tour is a tourism staple in Colorado. The company first gave unofficial tours of the brewery in the late 1940s. In 1951, the tour was made a year-round function. More than a quarter million visitors tour the brewery each year, and each tour ends with samples of Coors beverages provided free of charge.

to work closely with Coors' distributors. He also appointed Everett Barnhardt as the company's general sales manager. Ad had a speech impediment, so Barnhardt took over most speaking chores at various state wholesaler conventions.

Barnhardt logged tens of thousands of miles on the company plane, a single-engine Ryan Navion. His bow tie, eyeglasses, crew cut and effervescent personality were well-known throughout Coors' growing distribution area.

In 1947, Coors instituted its annual sales meeting, which was held for many years in Room 5 on the third floor of the main office building. The original meeting consumed most of two days and included some 14 to 18 people from the sales and advertising departments.

These affairs were not all work. Social activities included luncheons and dinners held at Duke's, El Rancho or the Cosmopolitan Hotel. It was not uncommon for employees to display their talents on stage at these functions, including Bill Coors tickling the ivories and, at one memorable affair, with Ad accompanying him on drums.

In 1948, Coors turned an unofficial tradition into a public relations tool. Meetings with distributors often ended with a tour of the brewery. The company decided to organize a formal brewery tour during summer months led by a part-time guide. The tour was so successful that it was expanded in 1951 into a year-round event led by a full-time tour representative. Always thoughtful about appearance, Adolph Jr. dressed up the visitors reception area with

brass rails and tiles to keep it bright and shiny.

From the 1950s through the 1970s, Coors cultivated this personal approach to its public relations activities. The second floor of the office building became home to the Coors Theater, Bar Room and Lounge, built in 1950 to entertain the company's many business associates and guests. Drawing from Coors' advertising logo, the bar and lounge was dubbed the "Coors Waterfall Room." It featured a miniature waterfall display with live trees and shrubs. This theme figured prominently in other corporate marketing endeavors, such as the portable waterfall sign the company frequently lugged to conventions.

The Coors Theater comprised a stage and projection booth for viewing motion pictures, many produced by the company. *Seeds of Gold*, a documentary detailing the growing, harvesting and processing of Coors' Moravian barley, and *Beer's the Name* "had real box office appeal," the first issue of *Caps and Taps* reported.

Caps and Taps was introduced in April 1950 as the brewery's communications pipeline to its distributors. Originally, it was only two pages and had no pictures. Only three issues were printed the first year for roughly 1,200 readers. By the time of its discontinuation in 1985, when the company switched its editorial focus to another house magazine, *Coors Courier*, the publication had a circulation of more than 6,000.

POSTWAR PROSPERITY

The 1950s were a decade of economic prosperity and new cultural phenomena. The average corporate executive earned $15,000 in 1950, and the higher wages translated into more money to spend and enjoy. Nearly everyone owned a black and white television and at least one car — typically huge boat-like automobiles with "tail fins."

Americans also drank more beer. Coors' booming beer sales had already motivated it to spread its

Visitors to Visit Coors this Summer

Out-of-Staters to Be Conducted Thru Golden Plant

Thousands of tourists from the "hot belt" states will visit Golden this summer, attracted by the opportunity to inspect a modern brewery. Adolph Coors Jr., announced yesterday that he would co-operate with the Hot Belt Advertising committee of Rocky Mountain Motorists, Inc., and would make arrangements to show all out-of-state visitors through the Golden brewery and malted milk plant.

This action of Mr. Coors will result, it is predicted, in bringing to Golden thousands of visitors from the dry states of Kansas, Nebraska, Texas and Oklahoma. None of have legal beer at this

C oors' waterfall logo
was incorporated in
1937, the same year it
introduced its famous
"Brewed with Pure
Rocky Mountain Spring
Water" slogan.
Through the years, the
waterfall — originally
depicting the Fish
Creek Falls in

Steamboat Springs,
Colorado — has been
altered to suit adver-
tising goals. Water is
the "most important
ingredient in beer,"
Adolph Coors, Sr.,
once said. Coors is
fortunate to use some
of the world's purest
and finest.

What's Up, Doc?

C oors' waterfall logo is nearly as
recognizable to Coors beer
drinkers today as its Castle Rock trademark. The waterfall logo, which depicted the Fish Creek Falls in Steamboat
Springs, Colorado, was incorporated in
1937, the same year the company
introduced its "Brewed with Pure
Rocky Mountain Spring Water" tag line.

During its post-World War II advertising campaign, the waterfall served the
company admirably. Portable waterfall
signs were lugged to distributor conventions and the visitors' lobby even
featured a miniature waterfall fountain.

In the 1970s, however, as Coors
pondered national expansion, a Coors
marketing executive thought the waterfall looked too much like — well, like a
rabbit. An artist was commissioned to
redraw the waterfall — hence, the
Coors waterfall logo of today.

These matchbooks
display various Coors
advertising logos and

wings in 1948 to Texas, the 11th state in its marketing region. In 1950, the year Coors discontinued the Export Lager brand — a heavier beer preferred by old-timers — to concentrate on sales of Banquet, production skyrocketed to 666,000 barrels. The growth stunned Coors' senior management. "Back in 1946, my father asked me what I thought the ultimate capacity of the brewery was," Bill Coors recollects.

"I said a million barrels. A cloud passed over his face, and he then told me I was dreaming. Yet, here we were, just four years later, well on our way to hitting a million." Only five more years would pass before Coors' production surpassed the one million barrel mark.

To satisfy rising demand, Coors needed to enlarge its facilities and purchase more up-to-date equipment. Bill Coors' background as an engineer served the company well in these endeavors, and the brewery gradually became the most technologically advanced in the nation, if not the world.

Ground was broken for a new malt house in 1950, and a new 200-foot-high grain building was dedicated two years later. At the ceremony, a flag famous in Golden history was raised. Thirty-three years earlier, Louisa Coors had presented the flag to returning World War I veterans.

Six-can cartons conceived and assembled by beverage distributors hit the scene in 1950, and the first load of palletized kegs left Coors dock two years later. Taking note of distributors' success with the six-pack, Coors introduced its own machinery in 1954 to produce and assemble the cartons at the plant. The composition of the cardboard six-pack won Coors top honors in the 1957 carton design contest sponsored by the Folding Paper Box Association.

Coors' advertising also displayed creativity during the decade. Trucks were painted

In the early 1950s, beverage distributors developed the practice of offering cans and bottles in packages of six. Although they did not invent the strategy, Coors distributors quickly adopted it as a customer-friendly means to sell more beer and in turn gave Coors the impetus to package Coors bottles and cans in six-pack cartons, introduced in 1954. In 1957, Coors' six-pack won top honors at a carton design contest sponsored by the Folding Paper Box Association.

Brewed With Pure Rocky Mountain Spring Water

Coors

America's Fine Light Beer

General Outdoor Adv Co

with the words "Brewed with Pure Rocky Mountain Spring Water" in gold letters, and bill-boards carrying this slogan sprouted like mushrooms in the West along the nation's burgeoning interstate highway system. The latter were especially imaginative, winning Coors first place for outdoor design in the 1957 National Highway Display Competition.

The brewery also sponsored road races and other professional tournaments, and it sent elaborate floats to state and city fairs and parades. Retail displays included flashing six-packs and waterfall signs that looked as if the water actually was flowing. These were so ingenious that Coors often bemoaned the practice of some retailers to plaster the company's signs everywhere. "[It] lowers the public's general opinion of us," *Caps and Taps* reported in April 1958.

Some marketing displays were particularly ambitious. One, for example, was too big to fit through

The Rocky Mountains conjure images of open prairies, pristine vistas and unbridled freedom — themes that appealed strongly to Americans. Coors capitalized on these feelings in its advertising during the 1960s, much as it continues to do today. Truck-sides and highway billboards spread Coors' message across the West. Coors' advertising efforts were recognized by the National Highway Display Competition in 1957, when Coors was awarded first place for outdoor design.

No Wonder They're Called "Floats"

On its way back from a Denver parade in 1953, a Coors tractor trailer carrying the company's elaborate float faltered, and the trailer broke loose from the tractor pulling it and slid into the fast-moving Colorado River. Within minutes, the trailer — emblazoned with bold "Coors" lettering — traveled downstream a distance of nearly a mile.

"We told the [driver] we were amazed at the lengths he would go to towards getting advertising free for Coors beer," *Caps and Taps* reported in one of its first issues.

In a postscript, the magazine added, "To all of you who have been inquiring — the Coors float is out of the hospital and is bigger and better than ever before."

The one that got away!

Coors' creativity when it came to point-of-sale and other display-oriented marketing was esteemed throughout the industry. The company created bar signs that incorporated backlit waterfalls that had the look of running water. Larger waterfall displays were lugged from one wholesalers' convention to another. One particularly large display couldn't fit through the doors of an exhibition hall. It stayed in the lobby, attracting more visitors than the more appropriately sized displays of other breweries inside the hall.

the doors of the exhibition hall at a wholesalers' convention. The company had to leave it in the hallway, where it attracted considerable attention.

In August 1953, a group of Coors distributors gathered at the brewery to discuss a new advertising medium — television. A few months earlier, Coors had sponsored one of the first TV series to air in Colorado — *I'm the Law*, with tough-talking actor George Raft. The show was a hit, and it prompted Coors and the distributors to pour more advertising dollars into television.

Coors' early television commercials were primarily voice-overs that aired during the opening and closing credits of *I'm the Law*. They carried background music by some of the brightest talents of the day, including Tommy Dorsey, Duke Ellington and Benny Goodman. The bandleaders were playing in nearby Denver and decided to take the Coors Brewery Tour. When Coors' advertising department found out, they quickly contracted their musical services.

While Coors' inventive advertising no doubt contributed to sales, had it not advertised at all, sales still would have climbed. Said a former executive, "We could have sold our beer in baggies!"

After production passed the one million barrel mark in 1955, Adolph Jr. again asked Bill Coors to estimate the brewery's capacity. "I said I believed we could produce two million barrels," Bill says, chortling.

"I then looked up at my father only to see the same cloud appear on his face."

TEAMWORK AND TITLES

Adolph Jr. and his sons ran the company during the postwar era as a team. "My brothers and I did have general areas of responsibility based on our particular strengths and skills," Bill says.

"Ad oversaw our early sales efforts, administration and raw materials program. Joe worked mostly at the porcelain company, and I basically ran the brewery. While we went about our separate endeavors, however, each day we tried to meet for lunch to discuss the company as a whole."

In June 1952, in a one-page handwritten memo, Adolph Jr. drew up management titles for each of his sons as follows: Adolph Coors III, board chairman of both Adolph Coors Company and Coors Porcelain Company; William K. Coors, president of Adolph Coors Company and executive vice president of Coors Porcelain Company; and Joseph Coors, president of Coors Porcelain Company and executive vice president of Adolph Coors Company.

Then, in a paragraph that provides insight as to Adolph Jr.'s philosophy of family business, he added that the titles "mean nothing and should not be displayed. We all have equal responsibility [to the company] as individuals and as a group."

One of the team's more difficult decisions in the

late 1950s regarded operations at the malted milk plant. Intense demand for Coors beer was stretching the brewery's ability to produce enough malt for both beer and malted milk. Thus, in 1957, the company decided to close down the malted milk plant. It had never been a profitable venture, but it had kept the company alive — and its employees working — during the dark days of Prohibition.

Ironically, when Coors Golden Malted Milk was discontinued, few employees took notice. "We were so busy making beer, it kind of slipped by," one former worker confessed.

Coors' malted milk plant kept the company's employees working through the difficult years of Prohibition and the Great Depression. Over the years, the plant diversified into many related milk products, including sweet cream butter. The motive was more altruistic than expedient. "We were looking to help depressed dairy farmers in the area, rather than make new profits," recalled George Golightly, a former plant employee. The malted milk plant was closed in 1957, shortly after this picture was taken, so the company could focus on its beer business.

After the repeal of Prohibition, Adolph Coors, Jr., personally invited the brewery workers union back to the plant. For the most part, relations between the brewery and Local #366 were peaceful, although disputes were not uncommon. Union workers here picket the brewery in the mid-1950s. A more serious strike in 1977, led to the eventual decertification of the union by its members.

LABOR TROUBLES BEGIN ANEW

As the country confronted yet another war — against the communist nation of Korea — battles of a different sort challenged Coors. "In 1951, the national brewery union sent a union business agent to Local #366 with the express purpose of instilling militancy into the union," Bill Coors says.

"This was to be the end of what had been, up until then, an ideal management-union relationship."

Although a strike by workers in 1953 was amicably settled within a week (the Coors brothers even invited strikers into the plant for free beer!), a subsequent strike in 1956 was more severe. The company

was stunned by the brewery union's attempt to organize the porcelain plant with the promise of wages equal to those of the brewery's.

Workers at the porcelain plant threw a picket line around the brewery in January 1956. Although the brewery workers had no dispute with the company, they refused to cross the picket line and report to work. The strike was long and hostile. After two months, the union backed down and left the porcelain plant alone. But the issue was not buried.

When negotiations opened at the brewery for a new contract in February 1957, the old animosities returned. The union wanted to negotiate wages and benefits equal to those of the national breweries. The company was willing to discuss these issues, but it also wanted to address issues raised by the porcelain strike, particularly the formation of the picket line and the violence it spawned. Coors insisted on a clause that would allow its production workers to cross a picket line without reprisals by the union.

"No brewery in American history has ever prevailed in a strike situation by shutting down operations and sitting the union out," Bill Coors explains.

"Industry competition is just too intense to risk what could be a devastating loss of market share. That's why it is a long-held tradition in the industry for the brewery union to allow a standby crew of union workers to keep operations going, providing management commits itself not to produce any beer with non-union workers."

Negotiations broke down, and in April a strike was called. While the union permitted the standby crew at first, when the strike persisted beyond the five-week mark, these workers were pulled. "There's no question in my mind that the union was seeking revenge for its humiliation over the porcelain strike fiasco," Bill asserts.

"They wanted to bring us to our knees — even if that meant shutting us down forever. I remember my father calling me and my brothers into his office during the strike and saying, 'Boys, we're shutting the doors for the last time.' He was convinced we could not operate without a union label on our bottles."

The company persisted, trying something that had never before been attempted in the brewery industry — operating with temporary workers. Many were chemical engineering students from the Colorado School of Mines and the University of Colorado. Working with Coors management, they produced record quantities of beer in the summer of 1957 — much to the union's chagrin.

"This was tantamount to declaring an all-out war with no holds barred," Bill says. A court injunction obtained by the company allowed a near-normal flow of materials, products and people in and out of the brewery.

As the strike neared the four-month mark, Coors announced it would hire permanent replacements for the striking workers. The strategy broke the picket line, as well as the hold of the national union on Local #366. The strike was settled, and on August 18, 1957, after 117 days of no work, striking employees began to return to their old jobs.

"A staunch union employee told me right after the strike that the company couldn't do anything right," Bill Coors recalls.

"I asked him why he stayed at Coors, then, if everything was so bad. He replied, 'If I could find a job half as good as this one, I'd quit.'"

ALUMINUM CAN DO

As it struggled to breach the divide with its employees, Coors' engineers were hard at work leading the company into the future. In 1957, led by Bill Coors, the engineers began researching the feasibility of a recyclable aluminum container for beer.

At the time, tin was the can of choice for the beverage industry. The metal, however, gave beer an unpleasant aftertaste. Tin cans also leaked, and they created environmental problems. Coors engineers had another concern — they wanted to find a way to

brew beer without pasteurizing it.

"We had this idea that pasteurizing beer affected the taste," Bill Coors says. "If you're not going to pasteurize beer, then you have to produce a beer that is devoid of any kind of microorganism. A challenge was to come up with a can that could be sterilized to prevent spoilage."

The engineers thought aluminum would fit the bill, but at that point, the metal had never been used for beverage containers. Moreover, there was enormous resistance from can manufacturers and competing breweries committed to the existing can technology.

Bill Coors did not let the criticism sway his

A Princeton-educated chemical engineer, Bill Coors worked many years developing an all-aluminum beverage container, which he proudly introduced in 1959. The cans previously used altered the taste and quality of the beer. "If your whole being is dedicated to quality, it just hurts to put a fine product in a very deficient package," Bill Coors says.

resolve. He travelled to Europe to observe "impact extruded" aluminum container manufacturing processes, and he imported the necessary equipment to experiment in Golden. Although his research experienced a high failure rate and many aluminum container manufacturers insisted he was chasing a will-o'-the-wisp, he and other Coors engineers continued to refine their processes.

After many setbacks, they finally succeeded, developing a seamless, two-piece impact extruded aluminum can in 1959. The seven-ounce container consisted of the can itself and the lid — a pony-sized can "perfect for the ladies, who loved it," Bill says. The company retailed the new cans in eight-packs for sale in Colorado, promising consumers a penny for every can returned to the brewery — the beginnings of the recycling revolution.

Several years passed before the brewery was able to convert entirely to aluminum containers. Even so, the cans represented a significant first for both the beverage and metal industries. For his tireless efforts pioneering the first all-aluminum beverage can, Bill was named "Man of the Year" by *Modern Metals* magazine in 1959. "Bill Coors and the aluminum can he developed are symbols of achievement and hope for [aluminum] in a market that grows in importance with each passing year," the magazine cheered.

Coors' engineers immediately began to research the possibility of producing much larger aluminum cans. Their plans also included "closing the loop" — melting used cans to cast sheet aluminum from which new cans could be manufactured. Bill returned to Europe in the mid-1960s and bought a revolutionary, yet-untested, technology for continuously casting rigid sheet aluminum from molten aluminum.

In 1966, a new can production system was designed using the technology. The old seven-ounce containers were phased out and discontinued in the early 1980s, and more standard-sized cans were introduced. To produce the cans, Coors formed a

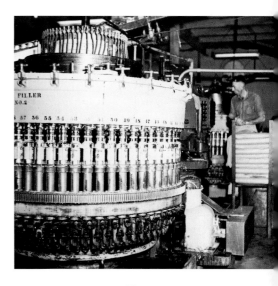

Bill Coors went to Europe to study the "impact extruded" process of manufacturing aluminum containers as he was developing the aluminum can. Though others in the industry laughed at his efforts, the aluminum can eventually became the container of choice for most beverage manufacturers and gave a boost to the aluminum industry as well.

Prior to Coors' invention in 1959 of the sterile fill process for brewing beer, all packaged beer in the world was pasteurized before sale. Although pasteurization killed any micro-organisms that were present in beer, it sorely affected its taste. Coors' unique process did away with pasteurization. Special filters removed microorganisms, and all brewery equipment and facilities were kept in a sterile environment. Constant monitoring of the system ensured optimal quality.

new division within Coors Porcelain Company. It later became a separate, wholly owned company — Coors Container Company.

STERILIZED, NOT PASTEURIZED

Now that an all-aluminum can was available, Bill Coors embarked on phase two of his plan — producing unpasteurized beer. Bottled beer in America had been pasteurized since the early 1900s to kill bacteria and prevent leftover yeast cells from fermenting in the package after sealing. Like tin cans, however, pasteurization altered the fresh-tasting flavor of Coors beer.

In 1959, the company's engineers discovered and introduced what they called the Coors sterile fill process. To prevent the entrance of microorganisms

during brewing, beer is strained through a series of specialized cotton fiber filter pads. In addition, all pipes and tanks used during brewing are chemically cleaned on a routine basis. Finally, the product is monitored and tested for microbiological contamination during every aspect of its development.

"While the sterile fill process is tedious and costly," Bill Coors says, "it ensures the highest product quality."

As with any beer, Coors is at its finest when first packaged. After that, the flavor deteriorates because of time and temperature considerations. To retain peak brewery-fresh flavor for the longest possible time, Coors developed another revolutionary concept — controlled temperature marketing, now referred to as refrigerated marketing.

Coors' cans, bottles and kegs are filled at 34 degrees and kept cold until delivered to retail outlets. Once packaged, the beer is loaded directly from packaging lines into insulated railcars or refrigerated trucks for immediate shipment to distributors. The beer then is unloaded into a refrigerated warehouse. The last leg involves delivery of the beer to retailers, again in refrigerated trucks.

"At the time, refrigerated warehouses were unheard of in the brewing industry," Bill Coors says. "We convinced our distributors the idea had tremendous marketing potential, since it guaranteed Coors beer would be the freshest-tasting available. Our customers proved us right."

This remarkable series of innovations ushered Coors to the front ranks of the industry in terms of technological prowess and solidified the public's view of Coors beer as synonymous with product quality.

"You know, one of the toughest challenges after all these pivotal breakthroughs," Bill chuckles, "was figuring out how to put a label on a cold, wet bottle of beer! We did it, though, developing what we call a composite bag, which is simply a paper that has strong wet strength. And so it goes."

BUILDING FOR TOMORROW

During the 1950s and 1960s, the brewery buzzed with the sounds of construction projects. Every issue of *Caps and Taps* had a section devoted to these activities, which were ongoing and extensive. Among them were new grain and water storage facilities, a new brew house and malt house, a gleaming fleet of new trucks, state-of-the-art hops presses and new steam-heat malt-drying machines — the latter replacing old gas-fired kilns.

"I used to go home at night and have nightmares about that gas heater blowing up the whole brewery and taking half the town with it," Bill says. "So we came up with this idea for steam heat, which nobody had ever dreamed of doing at the time — except us, of course."

Funds earmarked for the projects came from retained earnings. Memories of Adolph Coors' debts following the Great Memorial Day Flood were not forgotten. Adolph Jr. promised he "would never borrow a dime" to expand the brewery, and he stuck to his word.

Fortunately, sales were through the roof, guaranteeing a steady flow of dollars. Indeed, the brewery had difficulty producing enough beer to satisfy demand. To cope, it requested in 1956 that distributors place orders at least two weeks in advance, rather than two or three days before, which many were doing.

Demand continued to skyrocket, escalating 25 percent in 1958, a year in which most other brands suffered market losses. The annual sales increases in the brewery's 11-state marketing region ranged from 5 percent to 60 percent that year, depending on the state. The brewery strained at the seams. "Any hopes or thoughts we might have had about addition of certain new territories that have been very interesting to us must be laid aside for an indefinite period of time," *Caps and Taps* reported.

"Our retailers [already are] running out of Coors. Even though this is a rough problem, I wonder if perhaps this sort of problem is not preferable to one of having a supply and no market."

In 1959, Coors' business shot up yet another 12 percent. Meanwhile, the industry's sales plummeted 6 percent. *Caps and Taps* reiterated the brewery's major concern: "Can we supply the needed amount of beer?"

As Coors moved into the next decade, the answer was a resounding "Yes!" Sharp minds produce sharp results, and in 1960, Coors doubled production to a then-astonishing two million barrels. But, as an old friend of Grover Coors — Jimmy Durante — used to say, "You ain't seen nothin' yet."

In 1960, Coors doubled production to a then-astonishing two million barrels. The brewery expanded over the decade but could rarely meet retailers' needs. As soon as their shelves were stocked with Coors beer, the cans and bottles flew out the door in customers' arms. By 1974, when this picture was taken, Coors was selling more than 10 million barrels per year.

FASTIDIOUSNESS AND FUN

To many former employees working at the company in the early 1960s, Coors was still a rather small family business. Most workers at the time were men — a mix of blue collar brewers and bottlers and white collar executives. The few women at Coors filled administrative positions in the main office. "We had to take a subservient role to the men," a female retiree recalled.

"Most of us were paid on an hourly basis — not a salary like most male employees. We also weren't allowed to dine with the men. Lunch for us was in a small room next to Bill's office, not that we ever complained about it."

Several retirees remembered how important it was to keep their desks tidy. "Adolph Coors, Jr., was just so meticulous. He would eye our desks, and if everything wasn't in place, he'd tell us to straighten it up," a former worker related.

"When you left at night, there literally couldn't be anything on the top of your desk — even your phone. You had to put it in your desk drawer. And you didn't dare leave a sweater on the back of your chair!"

Another recalled, "Everybody was on a first-name basis, but Mr. Coors was Mr. Coors. He was a very dignified gentleman, always in a sharp-looking dark blue or gray suit with a starched white shirt and high-button goatskin shoes. Oh, and a bow tie."

The bow tie tradition was carried on by Bill Coors, who was required to wear a tie in college. "I could tie that thing in the dark," he says. "As soon as my father died, however, I switched to four-in-hands. Shortly thereafter, I put them away, too, and just went tieless. I still hate to wear a tie, and so does everyone else in the family."

Bill is remembered by former workers in the 1950s and 1960s as "just one of the guys," said one retiree. "He used to come around and take our orders for lunch, writing them down on a piece of paper. Then he'd drive into town and pick it up. He always paid, of course."

TUMULT AND TRAGEDY

The 1960s were a turbulent decade full of promise and dashed hopes. John F. Kennedy became the nation's youngest president in 1960, only to be gunned down by an assassin's bullet in Dallas three years later. Astronaut Alan Shepard made the first U.S. space flight in 1961, but the deaths of three astronauts in a fire on a launching pad just six years later temporarily cancelled future manned space flights.

Tragedy also struck at Coors. At the age of 44, Adolph Coors III was kidnapped and murdered on February 9, 1960. Ad's murder prompted one of the biggest FBI manhunts in history, leading to the arrest and conviction of his killer in March 1961.

The entire company, indeed, the whole city of Golden, was stunned at the loss of this gentle man, a devoted husband and father of four. Several former employees recalled how difficult it was to look at Ad's empty desk, lined up against the wall next to Bill's and Joe's on the third floor of the main building.

The intense media scrutiny given both the murder and subsequent trial deeply affected corporate management. "We decided that in the future, obscurity would be our best security," Bill says. "We retreated as best we could from public view and actually paid people to keep the company out of the newspaper."

Even the family's philanthropic activities were kept under wraps. Pete Coors, Joe Coors' son, recalls as a boy looking at a plaque in a hospital that contained the names of donors. When he didn't see the Coors name, he inquired why. "Here we are," his mother replied, pointing. Her finger touched the word, "Anonymous."

CRIME STORY

The kidnapping and murder of Adolph Coors III, a 44-year-old husband and father of four children, on February 9, 1960, left an indelible impression on the Coors family, which retreated from public view for many years. The mystery that began with the discovery of Ad's abandoned car, its radio still running, ended with the arrest and capture of his killer, Joe Corbett, a former Fulbright scholar turned lifetime criminal.

The murder was not the first time the family was the target of opportunists or sociopaths. Adolph Coors, for example, stood face-to-face with a burglar one frightful night in June 1897. Working late in his office, the founder heard a noise outside his door. He opened it to encounter a man with his gun drawn. Coors slammed the door shut, ran to his desk and blew the plant whistle, sending the burglar to parts unknown. He was never captured.

Adolph Coors, Jr., also had a brush with near-tragedy. In September 1933, a plot to kidnap him for a $50,000 ransom was foiled when one of the conspirators was arrested in Kansas City, Missouri.

"His vehicle had a flat tire, and when the police came to help out, they figured out what he was up to," Bill Coors says.

"The police then set up elaborate plans to catch the rest of the kidnappers in the act. My father knew of the plot and told police he would allow himself to be kidnapped — even though he was scared to death. He just wanted to stop this dirty business!"

Though that plot was foiled, the "dirty business" did not stop. Ad's kidnapping and murder led to one of the biggest manhunts in FBI history. Seven months after his disappearance, a hunter found his body in the woods near Sedalia, Colorado. Two months later, Corbett was captured in Vancouver, British Columbia. A ransom note demanding $500,000 for Ad's return was traced to a Royalite typewriter Corbett had purchased, and paper found in his home matched that used for the note.

Corbett served 18 years and was released from prison in 1980. He lives in Denver, ironically, a few miles from the Coors brewery.

Adolph Coors III was only 44 years old when he was abducted in February 1960. The father of four and oldest of Adolph Coors, Jr.'s, three sons was loved and admired for his pleasant demeanor and kind disposition.

The NATURAL choice for your dog

GOLDEN CHOICE Dog Food

ANOTHER QUALITY PRODUCT OF ADOLPH COORS COMPANY
GOLDEN · COLORADO

Coors took a shot at selling dog food, just one of several enterprises based on brewery by-products. Others included B-6 vitamins and various farm animal feedstocks. The ventures were moderately successful, although the company later sold or curtailed the businesses. Today Coors focuses exclusively on the manufacture of beer and related beverages.

PICKING UP THE PIECES

In the wake of the tragedy, the Coors family threw their energies back into their work. The company led the brewing industry in dollars spent on capital improvements and equipment purchases.

A new railroad approach to the plant was constructed in 1960, as was a new reception area for visitors that featured "five bubbling fountains," *Caps and Taps* reported. Two years later, the company added a new bottle house and grain elevator.

New technology guided many improvements during the decade. For example, Coors automated its brewing process, installing a system designed by its own in-house engineers. It also purchased electronic equipment for beer ordering and shipment scheduling, jettisoning a 40-year-old filling system developed by Adolph Jr. Finally, a new automated can-body maker was designed by Coors engineers in 1968, eventually becoming the machine of choice on can lines worldwide.

The company also entered a pronounced period of diversification. It launched a program to convert brewery by-products into brewer's yeast and animal feed for general sale. The latter generated one of Coors' more unusual enterprises — the cattle feedlot business. Coors owned thousands of Angus steer in the 1960s and 1970s and even entered them in stock shows. The beef was later sold to packing houses for resale to restaurants and retail stores.

BOOM TIMES BEGIN

In the late 1960s, the nation was transformed by the war in Vietnam and the public divisiveness it generated. The baby boom generation came of age, and many publicly demonstrated their opposition to the war. Although he was much older, Bill Coors shared their outrage. "That war was our government's most irresponsible act — ever," Bill opines.

"Here we were supposedly containing communism thousands of miles away when we had Cuba right here in our own backyard and were doing nothing about it! I had a son who was almost of draft age, and let me tell you, I was not going to send him over there as cannon fodder."

As the nation's youth celebrated their independence and newfound political awareness in the late 1960s through demonstrations, "happenings" and enormous music festivals, Coors also had something to cheer about. Northern California and eastern Texas were added to the company's marketing area in 1966, helping to boost overall sales the next year past the four million barrel mark.

The record output — up one million barrels in just four years — lifted Coors from its position as the tenth largest brewery in the country to the seventh. Buoying the brewery's sales was good old American thirst — nearly 107 million barrels of beer down the hatch in 1967, an industry record.

In 1968, Coors amassed a sales volume of five million barrels, fifth-largest among U.S.-based breweries. A year later, Coors reached what it believed was its absolute capacity — six million barrels.

It was a premature assessment.

VERTICAL INTEGRATION AND GROWTH

The next decade began promisingly for Coors. The brewery produced more than seven million barrels of beer in 1970, elevating it to a position as the fourth-largest brewery in the country — an amazing accomplishment for a beer-maker with only an 11-state marketing region. In each of these states, except for Texas, where it did not sell statewide, Coors beer was the top seller.

The brewery industry entered a pronounced period of consolidation and competition in the 1970s. Several well-known breweries, such as Tivoli, shut down. Others merged or diversified into other fields to keep dollars flowing for advertising and capital improvements.

Coors expanded vertically. "We didn't want to be captive to the price and availability upheavals of businesses critical to the brewery or the porcelain plant," Bill Coors explains. In the early 1970s, the company formed operating units to handle packaging, energy and transportation. Although not directly related to the brewing process, all those Angus steer would form the basis of Coors Cattle Company.

The new companies pursued acquisitions within their respective industries. Coors Container, for example, bought Columbine Glass and Paper Packaging, while Coors Energy Company bought and leased several coal and natural gas reserves.

This strategy of self-sufficiency followed to the letter Coors' maxim: "The more we do ourselves, the higher quality we have." Indeed, the company made its own cans and bottles, used water from snow-fed springs on its own land, met most of its energy needs through its owned or leased coal and natural oil reserves and contracted farmers to grow its own hops and barley under Coors' stringent quality standards.

In addition, the company's engineering staff designed most of its machinery and equipment, which were assembled by Coors' construction workers, and its on-site greenhouse and nursery supplied the plants and flowers that adorned corporate offices. Coors also recycled everything in sight, from brewery waste to its aluminum display ads. As a local business newspaper reported, "Coors prefers to do its own thing."

Although many subsidiaries later would be sold or shut down, at the time their creation seemed especially prudent. When the energy shortage reached crisis proportions during the Middle Eastern oil embargo in the late 1970s and early 1980s, for example, Coors Energy Company supplied the brewery and porcelain plant with as much energy as they required.

Some corporate diversifications were less discerning, however. In 1973, Coors funded the forma-

tion of Television News Inc., which supplied line-fed video news to U.S. television stations. Although the company argued the news it supplied did not have a viewpoint, critics claimed it favored a right-wing perspective. Coors terminated the subsidiary in 1975, blaming the decision on TVN's continued losses.

As the company's offshoots competed for market share in their respective industries, the brewery decimated its own competition. Sales climbed year after year, reaching 9.7 million barrels in 1971 before ratcheting forward to 11 million barrels in 1974.

That year, Bill Coors also reached a personal summit of sorts, ascending to the top of Mount Kilimanjaro, Africa's tallest peak. "He was the oldest one of us by 10 years," reported a fellow climber. "He did nothing to train (for the climb), yet he made it all the way to 19,340 feet — and in good humor."

PUBLIC RECOGNITION AND SUPPORT

In June 1975, Adolph Coors Company became a publicly traded company on the NASDAQ stock exchange. Although the family's decision was driven largely by inheritance tax concerns, they knew the phenomenal growth of the company and its unher-

Denied participation in many sports because of a childhood bicycle injury, Bill Coors made up for the loss in the second half of his life. After a serious bout of executive burnout in the 1970s, Bill focused on his physical and spiritual health. He is a devotee of transcendental meditation, aerobic conditioning through stationery rowing and, until recently, mountain climbing. Bill became one of the oldest individuals to climb Africa's tallest peak, Mount Kilimanjaro, in 1974.

BREWED WITH PURE ROCKY MOUNTAIN SPRING WATER

Coors
AMERICA'S FINE LIGHT BEER

ADOLPH COORS COMPANY • GOLDEN, COLORADO 80401

Coors bottles through the years changed dramatically in shape, color and size. Early bottles were sealed with corks and covered with tinfoil and wire. These sturdy bottles were used to transport beer over large distances. Later bottles featured amber colored glass to block the damaging effects of sunlight, porcelain stoppers and, finally, the crown crimped cap. This display also shows the variety of products Coors has produced over the years.

alded position as the nation's top quality brewer from brew kettle to shelf made Coors' stock a sound investment. The public agreed; more than four million non-voting shares, at $31 each, sold in just a few hours.

As the company began its second century, a new generation waited in the wings to join their father and uncle in the family business. Joe Coors' sons — Joe Jr., Jeff, Pete, Grover and John — would lend their muscle to push Coors beyond its small marketing area into a national company. Their era also would be marked by assaults on the company's image. Union conflicts, multiple boycotts and an unrelenting media scrutiny of the company would dog it through the late 1970s and much of the 1980s.

At the time of the initial public offering, however, the 102-year-old Adolph Coors Company reveled in its astonishing success — the fastest-growth rate of any brewery in the country since 1968. "Here we were, this regional brewery at the height of our credibility and renown, sailing along smoothly year after year and capturing ever-greater market share," Bill Coors says.

"And then the dam burst."

It would be a long climb through the late 1970s and early 1980s before for Coors regained the stature it enjoyed in earlier years. A bitter strike, a protracted boycott and intensifying competition conspired against the company. Coors fought back with new products, a successful national expansion program, a contented union-free workforce, a burgeoning international marketing strategy and a creative advertising program. The brewery survived the difficult period and today is at the summit of its popularity.

CHAPTER FOUR

CATCH

✦

UP

J oe Coors' sons were raised on the brewery grounds in the 6-room cottage formerly occupied by their great-uncle Grover Coors, a house that was later razed to make room for the main office building of Adolph Coors Company. Joe Jr., Jeff, Pete, Grover and John Coors — the fourth Coors generation to enter the family business — were cut from the same cloth as their forefathers. They worked at the brewery in the summers, went east to study at Phillips Exeter Academy and on to study engineering at college. They enjoyed the typical pursuits of youth as the time neared for their entrance on the Coors stage.

They also were not above occasional mischief and pranks as young boys. "They used to play at the edge of the lake in what was then the loading area for keg trucks," Bill Coors recalls.

"To add to their mother's concerns, this was also where our rail-cars were loaded and unloaded. They liked to sneak up on top of an empty boxcar and make believe it was their fort. They didn't think we knew this, but of course we did.

prove themselves when they got out of college. Joe Jr., for example, didn't want any part of the company at first and went his own way. Jeff, who has a chemical engineering degree, was always on course as far as his future here. Pete, whose degree is in industrial engineering, also planned on the family business.

"My brother, Joe, and I acted as their mentors, guiding them or boosting them when they ran aground. On occasion the boys disagreed with us — just like my generation did with our father — but we always worked these things through.

"Over the years, they learned the ropes — knots and all. Joe Jr. and Jeff eventually moved over to Coors Technology Companies, while Pete stayed at the brewery and ultimately became its president. All of them are disciplined, driven and serious about their jobs and the future of this company.

"Although their father has retired to California, I work with them pretty much like my father worked with me and my brothers — as players on the same squad. And what a team we've been, confronting the new light beer revolution and the age of advertising; forwarding national and then international expansion; and overcoming a catastrophic boycott in the process. We made it, though, and we're stronger now than ever."

Jeff, Joe Jr. and Pete Coors join their father, Joe Coors, Sr., and uncle, Bill Coors, at the family mansion. This fourth generation of the Coors family helped guide the company through the turbulent 1970s and 1980s. They devised a strategy calling for the development of beer brands targeting different marketing segments, among them Coors Light, now the brewery's top-selling beer.

"The boys also liked to get lost down in the brewery's cellars or play in the hills of sand deposited here and there for construction purposes. Their mother was always in a panic about where they were, which was unnecessary, since there was always somebody at the brewery keeping an eye out for them.

"Like my brothers and I when we came of age, the fourth generation wanted to

In 1975, the media gleefully reported a minor White House scandal — Secret Service agents for President Gerald Ford apparently smuggled several cases of Coors beer from Colorado to Washington, D.C., aboard Air Force One. The story was greeted with some amusement and no more than a collective shrug by the public. After all, who could blame the president — Coors beer was America's best.

Consumer appeal was so high at the time that the company actually rationed the beer it produced. Ironically, the empty grocery store shelves only enhanced Coors' cachet. "We didn't need much marketing at the time," Bill Coors says. "The beer just sold itself."

Not for long.

A new light beer craze fostered by the Miller Brewing Company — and advertised like no other beer before it — took Coors by surprise. The company's torpid response affected its market share, which melted away like ice in July. Adding to the company's woes in the 1970s was a long and painful strike by the brewery workers union and a 10-year boycott of its products by the AFL-CIO and various minority groups.

Fortunately, Coors entered the 1980s back on track, moving inexorably toward national distribution of its beer — even entering joint ventures overseas. The company experimented with several new brands, including the highly successful Coors Light. And it continued to fight an eventually successful battle against the boycott.

By 1990, Coors would rank number three among U.S. breweries. With the purchase of a brewing facility in Memphis that same year, the company would continue to enjoy a high rate of growth.

SALVOS FROM THE 1970S

Back in the mid-1970s, though, Coors seemed more likely to follow the last footsteps of so many other failing breweries at the time. "We underwent one of the most harmful boycotts ever attempted by organized labor," Bill Coors recalls, his blood rising.

"It seemed like there wasn't one bum rap they didn't hang on us, or one special interest group they didn't pit against us. It cut deeply into our market share."

It had been almost 20 years since the company last squared off against the union. Coors' relationship with Local #366 took a turn for the worse in 1974, when its business agent resigned and a new agent — who declared his intentions to bring Coors "to heel" — was hired.

In 1975, for the first time in the company's history, its annual production of beer was not sold out. The sales slump — Coors' first — forced it to lay off roughly 100 employees. It was quite a shock since the company took great pride in its "no lay-off" policy.

Despite this setback, contract negotiations between the company and Local #366 in 1975 were unsettling but not irresolvable. The union demanded a 10 percent wage increase; the company proposed a 5 percent increase, based on a previous increase it had granted only six months earlier. An agreement was reached.

The next round of negotiations, begun in November 1976, however, deadlocked after two

Coors beer had historically "sold itself," but intensifying competition in the 1970s caused the company to rethink its marketing efforts. The introduction of Coors Light in 1978 was the first new product Coors had developed in 20 years. Several other new brews followed throughout the 1980s and were supported by focused advertising efforts. By 1990, these changes had catapulted Coors into the number three spot among U.S. breweries.

THE DENVER POST
Warm, Sunny Highs: 79-84

Voice of the Rocky Mountain Empire
••• Final Edition / 25 cents

'New' Coors nation's No. 3 brewer

Workers take Stroh purchase in stride

Striking workers picketed the brewery in 1977 in an attempt to shut down operations. Though only 1,750 of Coors total work force of 7,200 were covered by collective bargaining agreements, the union wanted an agreement forcing Coors to permit its non-Local #366 employees to honor the picket line. The company refused.

months. At the time, 1,750 of Coors' 7,200 employees were covered by the company's collective bargaining agreements — most of them members of Local #366. Even though negotiations were at an impasse and no contract was in effect, the company granted employees a 7 percent pay increase and an improved benefits package.

Wages and benefits were not the union's key issues, though. Local #366 wanted an agreement that allowed employees to honor a picket line. It also had some technical disagreements with the company regarding seniority protection from layoffs and who got to work preferential shifts. The union thought the previous contract was overly favorable to management and found the new one offered by Coors even more disadvantageous. On April 5, 1977, a strike was called.

"It looked to me like a vengeance strike by the AFL-CIO to finally crush the brewery's independence," Bill Coors contends. Indeed, the information disseminated to the media by the AFL-CIO focused less on the contractual issues and quite a bit more on such seemingly unrelated matters as Coors' practice of using a polygraph when interviewing job candidates. Minutes of the contract negotiations make no mention of the polygraph — it was neither a bargaining point nor a strike issue — yet it became a central feature of the AFL-CIO's campaign to discredit the company. Even *Time* magazine reported

that Coors' use of a polygraph to "probe into the lives of job applicants" triggered the strike.

Coors maintained the polygraph helped it screen out substance abusers, dishonest persons and subversives, and did not invade privacy. Many other corporations also used a polygraph as part of their hiring procedures, including McDonald's and 7-Eleven. Nevertheless, the die had been cast.

As for the strike itself, the majority of the 1,472 union workers walked off the picket line and returned to their jobs within the first couple weeks of the strike. Those who didn't — nearly 500 employees — were replaced.

But Local #366 refused to concede. Six months into the strike, the union filed a petition with the National Labor Relations Board charging Coors with unfair labor practices. Union members were convinced a favorable ruling in the case would boost their chances of a settlement with the company. The NLRB demurred, ruling the charges lacked merit.

Opposition to the company was not confined to legal channels. Joe Coors received threats against his life, and five Coors distributorships in California and Colorado were the target of bombs. Two exploded, causing extensive damage to the facilities, but fortunately no injuries. Coors offered a reward for information leading to the arrest and conviction of the bombers. A terrorist organization, calling itself the New World Liberation Front, took credit for the violence. No arrests were ever made.

The strike dragged on for more than a year. Many workers made do with $25 a week in strike pay from the AFL-CIO, supplemented by food stamps or other work at half their former salaries and less. Some applied for welfare.

By May 1978, only about 75 to 100 union members were reported to be actively involved in the strike. The picket line was largely ineffective anyway — two other unions representing workers at the plant had contracts preventing them from honoring the line. Coors' trucks rolled safely in and out of the plant.

In December 1978, a union decertification vote was called for. Only those on the company payroll could vote, thereby eliminating any remaining workers on the picket line. The theme of the election — "Give Us A Chance" — reflected Coors' conviction it could work better with employees on a one-on-one basis than through an intermediary. Workers agreed: Approximately 94 percent of eligible employees voted — 71 percent in favor of the company. The union was soundly defeated.

After the strike, some workers reflected on the experience. "There was...no winner," one employee stated in the *Denver Post*. "I think the company and the union butted heads, and the poor working guy was in the middle."

TELEVISED TRIALS AND TRIBULATIONS

Although the strike was over, the pain lingered. A widespread ban on Coors products spearheaded by the AFL-CIO eroded sales and affected the company's viability. Bill Coors alleges the organization disseminated to the public a series of falsehoods and misinformation. "They claimed we discriminated against minorities, when in fact we'd received awards from minority groups, veterans organizations and others for our efforts to hire, train and advance minorities and women," he says.

Coors' internal records indicate its work force at the time of the strike included 13 percent minorities and 17 percent women. The company also had been certified as an Equal Opportunity Employer by the U.S. government prior to the walkout.

"The AFL-CIO further implied that Coors beer was unsafe because it wasn't pasteurized," Bill adds. "That was total bunk and they knew it. They also said we routinely subjected employees to illegal search and seizure and involuntary medical examinations — two other damning fabrications.

Depending on the audience, we were anti-abortion, pro-abortion, pro-gun control, anti-gun control, anti-Equal Rights Amendment, pro-Equal Rights Amendment. In short, we had done something to offend everyone."

The company published a series of paid newspaper and magazine advertisements refuting the allegations point by point. Female employees even went out into the marketplace in person to counter the anti-ERA, anti-abortion and anti-woman allegations. But the company's tradition of paying to keep it out of the news — a practice adopted after the murder of Adolph Coors III — left it ill-prepared to meet the full-court press. "We were naked in the marketplace," Bill Coors concedes. "And it was all our own fault."

Shortly thereafter, the company instituted its first truly modern public relations department.

Placard-carrying union members thinned in number as the strike dragged on. Ultimately, the majority of union workers on strike walked off the picket line and returned to their jobs. In December 1978, union members voted to decertify Local #366. Since then, three attempts by the AFL-CIO to organize Coors' brewery workers have failed.

Coors uses two-row Moravian barley, considered a superior grain to the standard six-row barley used by many other brewers. Ever since its founding 125 years ago, the company has stressed quality and excellence in the materials and equipment used, from the finest hops and purest water to the state-of-the-art fermenting tanks. A recent label for Coors Original, opposite, was redesigned to include images of the barley and hops that give Coors beer its sought after taste.

FUEL TO THE FIRE

Just when it appeared things couldn't get worse, *60 Minutes* knocked on the door. Mike Wallace, the veteran anchor of the television program, came to interview Coors management in 1982.

With a friendly smile, Bill Coors told him, "Our books are open to anybody, Mike. Anybody can come in here and they can determine for themselves exactly what we do...how we make our products, what our hiring practices are. I know of no other company other than ours that has completely open books."

The *60 Minutes* crew met with an overflow crowd of employees in Coors' sixth-floor auditorium. Workers finally had an opportunity to tell their

organizations ever to receive a favorable report from the hard-hitting television program, seen by an estimated 42 million people. In his closing remarks, Wallace concluded that "Coors had been a victim" of a smear campaign.

"The show dispelled many untruths," Bill Coors says today. "In a way, it was our vindication."

LITE BEER BLUES AND BRUISES

Unions weren't the only problems confronting Coors in the 1970s. While the company's attention was diverted by the strike and boycott, its competitors attacked from the flanks with new beer brands touted by multimillion dollar advertising campaigns.

Leading the charge was the Miller Brewing Company. "After Philip Morris bought Miller in 1970, Miller developed marketing expertise that it delivered to the public in such a way that it literally overwhelmed the industry," Bill Coors says. "We found out — too late as it turned out — that people could be lured away from our product by massive expenditures of advertising money."

In 1976, Coors spent $9.8 million on advertising; Miller spent $50 million. Much of that money was earmarked for Miller's new beer brand — Miller Lite, a lower calorie beer that its advertisements announced was "less filling but tastes great." While Coors always billed its Banquet brand as "America's Fine Light Beer," the beer's calorie count — though lower than competitive premium beers — was nowhere near as low as Miller Lite.

Anheuser-Busch, the nation's biggest brewer, responded with a lighter version of Budweiser called Natural Light. Coors decided to stick with Banquet as its "light" beer — a decision that proved disastrous. Both A-B and Miller targeted Coors' marketing region and nipped away at its once impressive share.

In the state of California, for example, then Coors' largest market, the company plunged from a 37 percent market share to 22 percent between 1975

side. One woman stood up with her hard hat in hand and told Wallace about her non-traditional job in construction. Another employee, of Hispanic descent — asked if he had been "bought off" by the company — responded that if a good job with good pay and good benefits meant being bought off, it was okay with him.

As it turned out, Coors was one of the few

and 1977. Coors' overall production dropped by one million barrels in 1977, a far cry from the stunning increases of the early 1970s. That year, Coors reported the greatest sales percentage decrease in its history — a $9 million plunge in net income.

All across the West, Coors was getting creamed by the light beer rage. Sales of Banquet fell each year between 1975 and 1980, while Miller Lite sales zoomed upward an average of 36 percent during the same period. The myth of Coors' invincibility was shaken to the core. The mystique was fading.

ONLY ONE PLACE LEFT TO GO

Coors' management and marketing department realized changes were in order to prevent total ruination. Leading them in the effort was Pete Coors. Tall, lanky and unassuming like his father, Pete was the company's senior vice president of sales and marketing in 1978. He had undertaken the company's first market research in the early 1970s and had guided the building of its first modern marketing department.

"There was an attitude here in the mid-1970s that we could do no wrong," a tieless Pete Coors says from his modest office in Golden.

"That got me nervous. For example, we had invested in these press-tab cans that consumers didn't like, but the feeling among many in the company was that the beer was so good people would use their teeth to tear the cans open. Here we were the most sophisticated brewer in the country as far as production, and yet we were among the most unsophisticated as far as marketing and finance. We didn't even put our general ledger on computer until 1974."

Pete was the first member of the Coors family to grasp that the beer industry was moving toward market segmentation. He and his older brother, Jeff, sketched out a comeback plan for the brewery. Rather than defend Coors' market share with

Banquet alone, they planned a series of new beers aimed at different markets.

In 1978, after a year of product testing and consumer research, Coors introduced its first new beer in 20 years — Coors Light. The going had not been easy.

"There were some sharp disagreements about brewing a lighter beer," Pete Coors recalls. "Some members of the family wanted to continue to advertise Banquet as our light beer. If we did that, though, where would that have left consumers of heavier beers? It soon became clear to us all that the fastest growing segment of the industry was low-calorie beer, and that's where we aimed our marketing efforts."

Now that it had a light beer to pit against the competition, Coors needed a comparable advertising effort. The company hired on several established advertising pros to develop a strategy. Shortly thereafter, Coors Light was introduced to the public in what was then the most prolific advertising campaign in the company's history. Television and print ads trumpeted: "Something no other light beer has — the real taste of Coors."

Sales and marketing were elevated to positions of greater importance within the company. Coors' marketing department expanded to 40 executives in 1979, and the advertising budget more than doubled from $15 million in 1977 to $33 million

Coors' novel press-tab openers were designed to eradicate the environmental problems caused by ring-pull "pop-tops," which were fouling parks and beaches, not to mention city dumps. Though altruistic in design, some consumers found it difficult to use the press tab. Eventually, Coors introduced stay-on can openers. Coors Light, left, was a response by the company to the successful low-calorie beers of its competitors. Ironically, the first cans of Coors Light featured a similar design to Coors' other beer, Banquet. Customers had trouble distinguishing Coors Light from Original Coors, so the company's quick solution was to remove the buff-colored background. Once the cans were left in their natural silver state, sales of the "Silver Bullet" shot through the roof.

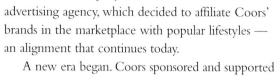

in 1978. The company hired its first full-service advertising agency, which decided to affiliate Coors' brands in the marketplace with popular lifestyles — an alignment that continues today.

A new era began. Coors sponsored and supported professional basketball, baseball, hockey and other major sports events. It signed golf superstar Lee Trevino for a series of personal appearances and exhibitions. New ad themes proliferated — "Taste the High Country" and "Coors, Make It Yours," for Coors Banquet; and "The Surprise is How Good It Tastes," for Coors Light.

Despite the spirited effort, sales of Coors Light started slowly. The company had packaged the beer in a buff-colored can similar to the can it used for Banquet, which confused consumers. After a few months of so-so results, Coors realized it had to do something immediately to differentiate Coors Light from Coors' original brew, Banquet. "Not wanting to waste months redesigning the can," says Bill Coors, "I suggested simply removing the buff-colored printing plate from the Coors Light cans." The simple silver-toned can did catch people's attention. Customers started calling Coors Light the Silver Bullet. Bang! Sales shot through the roof.

Coors entered the 1980s with a bang, advertising heavily on televised sports programs, from baseball to professional auto racing. This sports connection eventually led to the construction of a brewery inside Coors Field, home of the Colorado Rockies. Pete Coors shares a round of beer from The SandLot Brewery, above.

CEO Pete Coors typifies the rugged outdoors image imparted by Coors throughout its 125-year existence. An avid runner, Pete has competed in marathons and other running events. He continues to practice a healthy lifestyle, whether it be running in the foothills of Golden or working out at the company's Wellness Center, one of the nation's first corporate health facilities, created in 1981.

The Shot Heard
Round the World

The Silver Bullet advertising theme is recognizable today to beer drinkers from Portland to Potsdam as touting one of the world's finest beers — Coors Light. Yet, it might not have been so.

Back in the 1980s, the company was looking for a new ad line to advertise Coors Light. Serendipity intervened in the form of a phone call. Bill Coors had recently talked with his daughter, Maggie, at college. "She said, 'Dad, you know what everybody here at school calls Coors Light? They call it the Silver Bullet,'" Bill recalls. The expression derived from the telltale silver color of Coors Light cans, a rarity back then.

"After I hung up the phone, I got pretty excited," Bill notes. "When we had an advertising strategy session later that week, I brought up what my daughter had told me. I said, 'Why don't we capitalize on something that already has growing name recognition in a large segment of the marketplace? Let's call Coors Light the Silver Bullet!' To be honest, there wasn't much support, but I pushed it through. I knew we were onto something."

Thanks in part to the Silver Bullet theme, Coors Light is the third-largest selling light beer and the fourth-largest selling beer of any kind in America today.

REACHING OUT ACROSS THE LAND

Coors deemed 1978 its "Year of Change." It undertook a series of strategic steps to reposition the company in the marketplace. More money was invested in research and development of new brands, each brand aimed at a specific market, such as individuals in the military or young adults.

Coors also began a long-range program of enlarging its marketing region. Had Coors not made the decision to become a national company, it may not have survived. "Coors was losing market share rapidly in the West," says Jerry Steinman, publisher of *Beer Marketer's Insights*, an industry trade magazine. "Miller and Anheuser-Busch were devoting more and more advertising and marketing dollars to stealing its market share, aiming directly at Coors' heart. Looking back, if Coors had not expanded, it would have had to sell out to a larger brewery. There's no question national expansion was the prudent — indeed the only — decision." Late in 1976, Coors expanded into the states of Montana and Washington and into Nebraska, Iowa and Missouri the following two years. Each time it set its sights on a new state market, applications for distributorships flooded in. In Missouri, for example, Coors received more than 1,600 bids for fewer than 10 wholesale outlets.

As competition intensified in the industry, Joe and Bill Coors announced their intention in 1978 to expand the company's marketing area by two to three states a year until the company reached full national distribution. "The expansion program was really a defensive move to stay alive," Bill Coors says.

"We were in a small marketing region that was being chipped away by our competitors. Had we stayed regional, they would have chopped us into pieces. We had to go national, even though we

Coors Light is one of the world's largest selling beers of any kind, embraced particularly by the young as their brew of choice. The brand has been advertised with an eye toward this market segment. In Coors' 125th year, for example, several innovative television commercials aired featuring young people enjoying outdoor fun with the Rocky Mountains as their playing field.

Lining Up to Deliver

When Coors began its slow march across the United States, individuals and businesses lined up for a license to become a Coors distributor. In some states, it was not uncommon for thousands of applicants, some of them well-known personages, to request a distributorship.

When Coors moved into South Texas, for example, the petitioners included several ex-astronauts, a former Texas governor and even Vice President Spiro Agnew, just out of a job. The company interviewed them all. "It was my job to screen the vice president," recalls Ken Golightly, a Coors retiree.

"Spiro was perfectly charming, but I decided to pass on him. We wanted someone who would be involved in the business on a day-to-day basis, and I just didn't think he fit the bill."

Instead, the astronauts got the nod. Alan B. Shepard and his friend and former boss Captain Robert "Duke" Windsor were awarded one of the Houston distributorships. Another astronaut, Charlie Duke, was given a distributorship in San Antonio.

realized it would cost hundreds of millions of dollars."

Coors crossed the Mississippi for the first time in 1981, entering the states of Louisiana, Mississippi and Tennessee. Ten years later, the journey was over — Coors was a bona fide 50-state brewer.

It also was a brewery with only one brewing facility. The company realized the Golden brewery, even though it was already the world's largest, would be hard-pressed to meet the demands of a national marketplace. "When we reach the 25 to 27 million

Taste Washington quality in every Coors and Coors Light.

The quality of hops, the vine that gives beer its customary bite, is as critical to the taste of beer as the purity of the water or the variety of barley, and Coors uses only the finest. Although the founder used imported German hops to brew the first Coors beers, the brewery today imports hops from carefully selected farmers in neighboring states in the Northwest.

barrel plateau in Golden, we'll have to have another plant ready to go elsewhere," Joe Coors, Sr., stated in a 1977 interview.

An intensive search was undertaken for another brewery location. Joe, like his grandfather Adolph Coors, held to the notion that the company needed a location that was suitable for the task, namely a site with excellent water. In 1980, the company optioned two pieces of property that met the standard — one in North Carolina and the other in Virginia. Though the Shenandoah Valley site in Virginia later became a major Coors packaging center and finishing plant, ironically, neither of these original properties would become Coors' second brewery.

SUBSIDIARIES ACHIEVE SUCCESS

There were many changes in the style and sizes of Coors beer products in the 1970s. The 12-ounce bottle was introduced in 1974, replacing previous 11-ounce versions. Two years later, the old crimp cap began to give way to twist-off caps on most Coors bottles. Coors aluminum cans also underwent changes. Eight-ounce cans replaced seven-ounce cans in 1977, and the following year, the company introduced stay-on tab openers. The company's first 12-pack made its debut in 1978.

Nearly 9,000 employees worked at Adolph Coors Company as the 1970s drew to a close, making the company the second largest employer in Colorado. Bill and Joe continued to lunch together every day — except Thursday, which they set aside to entertain business dignitaries. The company still encouraged informality — coats and ties were rare, and employees and management abided by first names upon greeting each other.

The Golden phone book at the time had nearly a page devoted to various businesses with the name "Coors." The company owned as many as 16 subsidiaries, as well as manufacturing plants in four

A cold can or bottle of
*Coors can be had from
the neighborhood grocery
just about anywhere in
the United States — a
far cry from the early
1970s when Coors lovers
outside the distribution
area had to smuggle
theirs. Coors' national
expansion program
began in the mid-1970s,
and crossed the
Mississippi for the first
time in 1981, when it
entered the states of
Tennessee, Mississippi
and Louisiana.*

Soon after his introduction of the aluminum can, Bill Coors developed the technology and process for manufacturing new aluminum cans from used ones. By continuously casting rigid sheet aluminum from molten aluminum, Coors was able to complete the cycle of the cans. The new can technology was unveiled in 1966, launching the recycling revolution, and Coors' "Cash for Cans" program enabled it to become the first company to recycle more cans than it put into the marketplace in 1990.

states. Most of them sold their services primarily to the parent company. Coors Construction Division, for example, was the largest construction operation in the state, yet it worked only on Coors projects.

Others had modest non-Coors enterprises. For instance, Coors Transportation Company owned 150 trucks that moved Coors beer from the brewery to several distributors, but on return trips carried vegetables and fruits bound for the Colorado marketplace.

A few subsidiaries focused on the consumer market. Coors Food Products Company, capitalized in 1977, developed food products using brewery technology and by-products and even manufactured such snack foods as potato chips.

Other subsidiaries included Coors Container Company, which operated a paper packaging facility in Boulder, Colorado, as well as the largest single can manufacturing plant in the world in Golden. The plant's 2,000 workers forged nearly 3 billion cans in 1978 — for Coors alone. Coors' subsidiary Golden Recycle melted 157 million pounds of aluminum, most of which came from Coors' "Cash for Cans" program and the 254 recycling centers operated by its distributors. For every 100 cans put into the marketplace, 85 found their way back. By 1990, Coors became the first company to recycle more cans than it put into the marketplace.

Coors Energy Company supplied 55 percent of

JOE COORS

To many Americans in the 1970s and 1980s, Joe Coors was synonymous with the conservative ideals underpinning the presidency of Ronald Reagan, an administration he served with grit and fervor. To workers at the Coors Porcelain Company, however, Joe Coors was "Joe," the president who helped guide their once-small pottery into the world's largest producer of chemical porcelain.

Unlike brother Bill, who for the most part eschewed politics, Joe Coors took to it right away. He backed Republican

Governor Barry Goldwater in his bid for the presidency in 1964 and was himself elected a Regent of the University of Colorado in 1967. In the 1970s, Joe helped found and fund the Heritage Foundation, a Washington-based conservative think tank. Joe also served in an unofficial capacity on President Reagan's famed "Kitchen Cabinet" and has been a close, personal friend of the president since 1967, when they met for the first time in Palm Springs. "I was completely captivated by the man," Joe recalls. "He impressed me as a great leader, and I have stuck with him ever since."

Tall, steady and quiet like his father, Joe gives credit to his dad for his unswerving beliefs in the American free enterprise system. "He was a very hardworking person who believed wholeheartedly in the principles of freedom, liberty and opportunity in

Joseph Coors, Sr., piloted Coors Porcelain Company while his brother, Bill, focused his attention on the brewery. Both enterprises, though split into two companies today, are leaders in their respective industries. Joe Coors also made a name for himself in politics, where he was a valued member of President Ronald Reagan's so-called "Kitchen Cabinet."

this country," Joe says. "He always reminded us that our grandfather came over here as an orphaned, penniless immigrant, and yet was able to build this company that we still have today. It instilled in me this great desire and hope that such freedoms and opportunities would last forever."

During his 41-year career at the company, Joe lived on the grounds, raising his family within the shadow of the giant brewery. His first job was working the clay pits west of Golden, where miners dug the raw material for the porcelain company's products. Later, his background as a chemical engineer helped refine the technology behind Coors' cold-filtered beer manufacturing system, which he created with his brother, Bill. The brothers also launched the first large-scale recycling program in America, when they offered one cent for the return of Coors' seven-ounce aluminum can in 1959. Joe also led the search for Coors' second facility, Shenandoah.

Although Joe retired from daily management at Coors in 1987, he remains on the company's board of directors. He lives today in the Southern California area.

Of its many beer brands in the 1980s and 1990s, one in particular (besides Coors Light) has captivated the buying public — the George Killian's line of beers. William George Killian Lett, the bearded Irish fellow below and seated by the Irish Sea drinking his favorite brew with a fellow admirer, sold his recipe for the beer to the Coors brewery in 1981. Killian's remains a top seller today.

the company's natural gas needs via its own reserves and a 30-mile pipeline. The natural gas fired the kilns at Coors Porcelain Company and the glass and can plants. In January 1977, at the height of the energy crisis, the company won an Energy Conservation Award from the U.S. Federal Energy Administration for significant energy consumption reductions.

Coors Porcelain Company continued as the industry leader, manufacturing a wide range of products that included seal rings for the auto industry and lightweight bulletproof vests for law enforcement agencies and the military. In 1979, the company acquired Alumina Ceramics, a large ceramics company in Arkansas. It also established Coors' first overseas subsidiaries in Singapore and Brazil, which manufactured ceramic products for the electronics and paper industries, respectively.

NEW DIRECTIONS IN THE U.S.A.

In 1980, Ronald Reagan was elected the nation's 40th president and the Republican Party regained control of the Senate for the first time since 1964. Joe Coors was a longtime backer of the former California governor and had served as a Reagan

delegate at the 1976 Republican convention. During Reagan's first administration, Joe served as an advisor on his "Kitchen Cabinet."

The company took a lot of heat during the 1980s for Joe's conservative political views, particularly his support of the Nicaraguan Contras and the Heritage Foundation, a conservative think tank. Joe also voiced stiff opposition to federal red tape and government meddling in free enterprise. "Like everybody else, Joe and I have distinct political views," Bill Coors says.

"These positions, however, have absolutely nothing to do with Adolph Coors Company. Politics is a personal thing; a business, on the other hand, must remain apolitical. The brewery did not support these causes, yet it was tarred and feathered for them anyway by the radical liberal elements in this country. All we can do is accentuate the positive and ignore the negative."

As it continued to debate the relative merits of building a second brewery in Virginia, Coors began an aggressive expansion program at the Golden brewery. The objective, outlined in the company's 1980 annual report, was to reach a brewing capacity of 20 million barrels by the mid-1980s, financed entirely through internally generated funds. This was almost double the 12.9 million barrels produced in 1979.

The company spent more than $600 million in capital improvements during the 1980s on new malt houses, a five-story office complex, a Wellness Center and health facility, several parking lots and other facilities. To build these projects, Coors Construction required a force of some 650 workers.

The company continued its strategy of developing beer brands suited to different market segments. Super-premium beers were the fastest growing segment of the brewing industry, and Coors took aim at this market with a new beer — Herman Joseph 1868. The name commemorated the two middle names of Adolph Coors, Sr., and the date he set foot in America.

Coors Porcelain Company today is part of ACX Technologies, a wholly owned company separate from Adolph Coors Company. Seen here in hard hat is Joseph Coors, Jr, who, with his brother Jeff, helped build this company from the remains of a failed pottery into the world's largest producer of advanced technical ceramics, used in the manufacturing of a wide range of products — from spark plugs to uranium insulators.

*J*eff Coors, made president of Adolph Coors Company in 1985, took the helm of ACX Technologies — alongside brother Joe — when it was spun off from Adolph Coors Company. Jeff was a major force in the late 1980s diversification strategy that saw Coors acquire several technology-based companies and provided vision and leadership in developing the subsidiaries, including Golden Aluminum Company, Graphic Packaging Group, Coors Ceramics and Golden Technologies, which made up ACX.

Herman Joseph's was closer to the robust taste of the original beer brewed by the founder. It was successfully test-marketed in 1980, in six cities within Coors' marketing region. In later years, the brand underwent several changes in taste and look, including a stint with national distribution, but eventually was pulled from the market.

Another new beer — George Killian's Irish Red — was successfully test-marketed in 1981, and rolled out in several states the following year. The recipe for the brew — the first red beer in the United States — was concocted by a bearded, fanciful fifth-generation brewer from Enniscorthy, Ireland, named William George Killian Lett. The beer remains a top seller today.

Coors Banquet underwent a name change to Coors Premium in 1980, to better position it as a premium beer (the name Banquet was later restored). Coors Light, meanwhile, took the marketplace by storm. Sales escalated 35 percent between 1980 and 1981, and the beer's sales climbed steadily until it eventually became the number one light beer in many markets.

Coors also turned to new leadership. Pete Coors was appointed divisional president of sales, marketing and administration, and Jeff Coors was appointed divisional president of the operating and technical divisions.

"The infusion of youthful talent at the top of the company is important to our growth and to the continuation of family leadership," the 1981 annual report stated. Bill Coors remained the company's chairman and chief executive officer, while his brother, Joe, continued as president and chief operating officer.

Despite these leadership changes, expanded facilities and the success of new brands such as Coors Light, volume dipped below 12 million barrels in 1982, the first time since 1975. It was clear that the challenge from competition was tougher than ever. The company responded with a new advertising campaign focused on the company's national expansion into new markets: "The Best of the Rockies is Here" and later "The Best of the Rockies is Yours." Advertising themes linked to the concept included "Turn It Loose with Coors Light"; "Taste the Difference Time Can Make" (promoting Herman Joseph's); and "Made for the Way You Really Like to Drink Beer" (Coors Premium).

Sales and marketing efforts were enhanced in the important young adult market, and efforts were made to create improved awareness of Coors beer among African Americans and Hispanic Americans. The marketing campaign and expansion to the Southeast proved profitable. In 1983 — 50 years after the repeal of Prohibition — the company reported the highest profits in its 110-year history.

Coors' barrel sales jumped 15 percent to 13.7 million barrels, while the beer industry's barrel sales fell an average of 1 percent. Coors Light became the nation's number two light beer and number ten for all beers, while the flagship brand, now called simply "Coors," became the number two selling beer in Coors' 28-state marketing region.

Coors continued to focus on advertising. On a per barrel basis, Coors spent more on advertising in 1985 than any other U.S. brewer — $138.7 million. New ads included "Coors is the One," "Killian's Red, Instead" and the groundbreaking "Silver

Bullet" theme for Coors Light. Forty-four states marketed the brewery's beers coast to coast.

New subsidiaries also dotted the landscape, including Coors Packaging Company, Coors Biomedical and Coors Distributing Company. Golden Recycle Company introduced CanBank — the first automatic recycling machine paying cash to the public for used cans. The company's aluminum mill in Fort Lupton, Colorado, recycled the cans into sheet stock, from which new can ends were cut.

NEUTRALIZING A NEGATIVE IMAGE

Coors carved a market share wherever it could in the early 1980s — despite the ongoing boycott. Media scrutiny of the company dwindled and then, on February 23, 1984, returned with unprecedented aggression.

Bill Coors gave a speech that day to a group of Denver's minority business owners. As always, Bill spoke extemporaneously and without notes. He touched upon the educational and economic challenges confronting immigrants and African Americans, citing the example of his grandfather, Adolph Coors, Sr.

The *Rocky Mountain News* in Denver quoted selectively from the speech in an article the following day headlined, "Coors calls Blacks 'intellectual inferiors.'" Bill was flabbergasted.

"My point was that African Americans had tremendous motivation to succeed, but had been limited in that regard because of economic oppression and the impact of that on their educational opportunities," he says.

The business owners who heard the speech did not question Bill's intent. A competing newspaper, the *Denver Post*, reported that the speech received hearty applause from the African Americans in attendance. It was a "damn good speech," one attendee stated in the article. Another remarked, "If he had

Coors is the one.

Coors enjoyed great success with advertising campaigns that targeted the young adult market, but the company did not stop there. During the early 1980s, Coors also introduced new ads designed to increase awareness of Coors beer among African Americans and Hispanics. In 1984, one article would threaten to undermine Coors' commitment to the minority community and customers. The company's persistent effort to set the record straight and a rapprochement forged by Pete Coors stemmed the tide.

Pete Coors signed an agreement with the AFL-CIO in 1987, which led to the end of the union's boycott of Coors products. Coors promised in return not to stand in the way of any union organizing activities by the AFL-CIO.

said what the story said he said, he would've been dead."

"It was a bum rap," Bill says. "I was irresponsibly quoted as saying Blacks are inferior. I did not say it and do not believe it."

Coors filed a $150 million libel lawsuit against the newspaper. Three years had passed before both parties settled the matter in August 1987. Coors dropped its suit in return for a printed letter of apology from the *News*. It reads: "Undoubtedly, the headline and certain references in the article could have been more precisely prepared and worded to avoid any misinterpretation."

Unfortunately, the harm had already been done. Newspapers across the country broadcast versions of the *News* story, deepening the rift between the company and minority interest groups. Coors needed to mend its fences.

In late 1984, Pete Coors forged a rapprochement with African American and Hispanic interest groups, agreeing to hire more minorities and signing two pacts calling for investment in Black and Hispanic communities — $325 million each. In return, Pete asked them to support the company in their communities.

The pact effectively mended Coors' relationship with the minority groups. Nevertheless, the overall boycott led by the AFL-CIO remained in force. In 1984, Coors was contacted by the National Education Association (NEA), which had just voted to support the boycott. With Coors' approval, NEA General Counsel Robert Chanin brokered contact with the AFL-CIO to find out what it would take to end the dispute. The labor group did not know. "The AFL-CIO had been caught up in implementing the boycott, not ending it," Chanin reported to the *New York Times*. Three years of negotiations led to the signing of a peace pact in 1987. That year, Pete promised the company would not interfere with a union-organizing drive at the brewery if, in return, the AFL-CIO called off the boycott.

Since then, three attempts by the Teamsters union to win union representation of Coors' brewery workers — once in Shenandoah and twice in Golden — have failed.

After more than a decade of bitter recriminations, Adolph Coors Company finally was free of controversy. All around it though, U.S. breweries were failing by the dozen. "Schlitz, Schaefer, Rheingold — big breweries in the 1960s and 1970s — suddenly gone," Bill Coors winces.

"The thing that set us apart was that we are a family of engineers. We know what it takes to make great beer, and that kept us alive during this dark period."

CLIMBING OUT OF THE BARREL

Coors quickly regained its confidence. 1985 was an extraordinary year, with more than 14.7 million barrels sold — an increase of eight percent over the previous year. Coors was one of only two U.S. brewers to post a volume gain.

So, they've asked you to boycott Coors beer

Before you do, consider these facts

On April 5, 1977, some 1,472 members of Brewery Workers Local 366 walked off their jobs at the Coors brewery in Golden, Colorado. (This union represented 39% all the employees at the brewery.) T... was called by the union leaders a... rejected the company's new co... proposal.

The strike had little effect. M... of the striking workers have r... jobs and the brewery is in ful... Although the company and u... repeatedly, negotiations rema... deadlocked.

Since the overwhelming maj... 366 members aren't striking, the ... now spreading false propaganda t... persuade consumers to boycott Coors b... We simply cannot allow these falsehoods ... to go unchallenged.

So, we've printed this booklet to make the truth known. We have an obligation to our valued consumers, distributors, employees, retailers, suppliers and shareholders to set the record straight.

For additional or more detailed information please write: Adolph Coors Company, Dept. 802, Golden, Colorado 80401. We'd appreciate hearing your views and will be happy to answer your questions.

Sincerely,

Bill Coors, Chairman of the Board
August 1977

HELP! BOYCOTT COORS

1985 also was a gold medal year for Coors Light, which moved three notches up to become the seventh most popular beer of any kind in America. Sales jumped 20 percent each year between 1984 and 1987, a remarkable achievement.

Over the next few years, several beverages were introduced, including Coors Extra Gold, a full-bodied beer; Colorado Chiller, an ill-fated attempt to capitalize on the booming wine cooler trend with a beer-based cooler; Winterfest, a seasonal beer similar to bock beer; and Keystone, a popular-priced beer with exceptional market appeal. Other brands, such as Killian's and Herman Joseph's, were rolled out in more states.

In October 1985, the brewery became an international competitor via a licensing agreement with Molson Breweries in Canada to brew and distribute Coors Light in that country. Coors also entered into a three-way joint venture with Molson and The Kaltenberg Castle Brewery in West Germany to form a separate, independent company — Masters Brewing. The new venture's first brand, Masters Beer — a higher-alcohol, lower-carbonation super-premium brew — hit U.S. test markets in 1986.

New subsidiaries also were unveiled. Coors BioTech Products Company, formed in July 1985, focused on a process to produce chemicals from the fermentation of corn. Grover Coors was the driving force behind the establishment of MicroLithics Corporation in 1988. Scott Coors, Bill Coors' son, was part of the MicroLithics team that produced sophisticated electronic components for military computers.

Other subsidiaries underwent changes. Golden Recycle became Golden Aluminum and Coors Porcelain Company became Coors Ceramics. Coors Packaging grew significantly, acquiring the business and name of Pennsylvania-based Graphic Packaging Corporation in 1988.

The company's structure was modified in 1987 to achieve greater customer identification and

Welcome Golden-Elkton Shenandoah Express

economies of scale. Coors BioTech, Coors Energy and Graphic Packaging were blended into Coors Technology Companies, while Coors Brewing Company focused on beer.

Management also changed. Jeff Coors became president of Coors Technology; Pete Coors assumed Jeff's previous title as president of the brewery; and Joe Coors, Jr., became president of Coors Ceramics. Bill Coors retained his title as chairman, but dropped his CEO title. Joe Coors retired, but kept his vice chairman position on the board.

Coors recaptured the number four spot among the largest U.S. breweries in 1987, passing Heileman. The company's new Shenandoah facility was up and running, with the first shipment of beer arriving that April. Three months later, the first cases of Coors and Coors Light rolled off the production lines for distribution in the East.

Coors' packaging facility in Elkton, Virginia, provides the company with more effective distribution of its products in the East. The facility, located in the heart of the Shenandoah Valley, offers some of the purest water in America. Beer is shipped in an unfinished state from the Golden brewery to the Shenandoah brewery in Virginia, where it is finished, packaged and then loaded on trucks and railcars for delivery.

As the brewery industry scrambled across national borders, Coors was in the forefront. In May 1987, the company inked a deal with Japan's Asahi Breweries to brew and distribute Coors' flagship brand in that country. Asahi agreed to follow the brewery's rigid quality control standards and use its special high-altitude barley, yeast and hops. More than 780,000 cases of Coors beer were sold in 1988, but continuing distribution and quality problems eventually caused the demise of the agreement.

The new brewery ventures and competitors who were jealous of Coors' Rocky Mountain heritage required a reappraisal of Coors' decades-old slogan, "Brewed with Pure Rocky Mountain Spring Water." The company opted to retain most of the legend, dropping the words "Pure" and "Spring."

*A*ctor Mark Harmon, known for his role on the popular St. Elsewhere television series of the 1980s, personified a new kind of beer drinker — conservative, self-reliant and restrained. As Coors continued its national expansion, the company's advertising featured more nationally recognized faces. Elvira, below, was Coors' "Mistress of the Dark" for many years. Jenny McCarthy was the reigning "Queen of Halloween" in 1997.

THE GO-GO 1980S

Innovation continued to be a hallmark of the company in the late 1980s, as it had throughout its history. Coors unveiled the industry's first toll-free consumer hotline in 1987, which answered consumer questions on everything from the ingredients used in Coors beer to the company's ad campaigns.

A new space marketing technology for distributors — the Star System — was unveiled in 1987. The software program helped distributors and retailers allocate adequate space in their facilities for Coors products. More importantly, it demonstrated that Coors beer was a high profit item relative to the space required to carry it.

Coors also invented the Concord can printer, an external can coating process that became the industry standard. In addition, a new stainless steel keg line introduced in 1984, filled 420 kegs an hour — the fastest in the business. And in 1988, Coors presented a recyclable alternative to kegs — the Party Ball. The small container was perfect for afternoon barbecues with the neighbors.

Originality also defined the company's advertis-

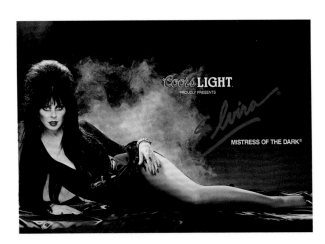

Coors took an equity position in an overseas brewery — Jinro Coors in South Korea — in 1991. The brewery is viewed as important to the company's expansion activities throughout the Pacific Rim. Pete Coors sits amid the new corporation's executives in this recent photo.

ing programs, a $250 million effort in 1989 alone. The rugged film and television actor, Mark Harmon, featured prominently in many commercials during the 1980s. Harmon had just the right look for the decade — clean-cut and solid. Sales improved.

As the 1980s roared their last, Coors moved one notch up in the list of top U.S. breweries to number three, a position it retains today. Sales nearly doubled between 1980 and 1990, and the company was recognized — once again — as having the fastest volume growth rate in the industry.

A NEW COMPANY FOR THE 1990S

Adolph Coors Company redefined itself in the 1990s as one of the world's best-known and best-selling breweries. During the 1990s, Coors decided to focus on its beer business and spun off its primary subsidiaries into a separate company concentrating on technology.

The reengineering was driven by the economic priorities of the era — intense focus on core competencies, maximization of shareholder value and

Now the national and even world headquarters of Coors' business, the Golden brewery is still the center of Coors brewing operations. Buses still pull up to the grand entrance full of curious tourists eager to see the method behind the mystique and sip a free sample of the end product.

increased globalization to attract more market share. To meet these objectives, the company decentralized corporate decision-making and elevated teamwork to a higher level. Coors also reconsidered its traditional policy of building only through retained earnings. For the first time since Adolph Coors, Sr., borrowed $90,000 to recover from the flood of 1894, the company turned to third parties to meet its new capital demands.

After a long search, Coors had found a source of equally superb water and its second brewery site. In 1990, the company purchased a Memphis brewery formerly owned by Stroh Brewing Company, and before it, Schlitz. A year earlier Coors had weighed the acquisition of several other Stroh properties, but no deal was consummated. Ironically, the Memphis plant had not been part of these negotiations with Stroh. Today, Zima Clearmalt, Coors Non-Alcoholic and the company's new line of Blue Moon specialty beers, are brewed there.

In 1991, Coors increased its international stature, taking an equity position in an overseas brewery — Jinro Coors in South Korea — and signing agreements in Australia and Scotland to expand into these markets as well. The board also restructured Adolph Coors Company into a holding company.

The rationale for the board's decision became clear in 1992, when one of the most significant events in the company's history transpired — the spin-off of the technology businesses into a separate public company, ACX Technologies, Inc. For the first time since 1908, when Adolph Coors, Sr., purchased a stake in a cement plant to diversify his fledgling company, Coors became totally focused on the production and distribution of beer products.

Another decision by the board in 1993 was equally historic — the appointment of the first non-family member as Coors' president. W. Leo Kiely III brought an impressive pedigree to the task

As Coors expanded its product line, additional brewing capacity became critical. After several years of searching, Coors selected a Memphis brewery owned by Stroh — primarily for the quality of its water — and purchased the facility in 1990.

— a career spent in the food industry, including a stint leading a division of the Frito-Lay Company. Today, he is a vital part of the Coors team as it reaches into tomorrow.

The stand-alone Coors Brewing Company, the primary subsidiary of Adolph Coors Company, entered a period of pronounced product research and development as the 1990s progressed. New beverages consisted of Coors Dry, the company's first beer in the "dry" category; Coors Non-Alcoholic; Zima Clearmalt; and Coors Artic Ice, the brewery's entry in the "ice" beer category.

Coors also redeveloped its Winterfest brand into the industry's first seasonal beer. In 1994, the year Bill Coors wrote that the brewery "spilled more beer than we made in 1939," the company purchased the El Aguila brewery in Zaragoza, Spain. Coors was awash in suds.

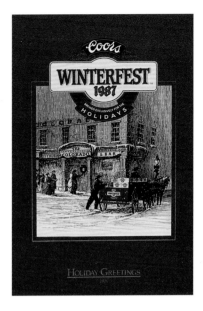

Leo Kiely III came to Coors as its new president in 1993, after a successful career piloting a division of the Frito-Lay Company. Kiely, a consumer products marketing expert who turned around the fortunes of the once-ailing potato chip concern, was a novice in the beer business. When offered to taste hops for the first time at the brewhouse, the new president put it in his mouth like chewing tobacco (customarily, hops is tasted with the tongue alone). The shock of the bitter taste stunned Kiely. Onlookers, including CEO Pete Coors, say he spent the next several minutes spitting pieces of hops into his handkerchief, his brow beaded with perspiration and his face crimson. "Leo took it all in stride," Pete Coors adds. Indeed, he works the tap like a pro.

Winterfest is a popular seasonal beer offered by Coors during the holidays. The beer is a throwback to the German bock beers of yesterday, including the early variety sold by Adolph Coors, Sr. Indeed, the recipe for Winterfest derives in part from an old mix written by the founder for his first bock beers.

Coors offered several beer brands in the mid-1990s, part of its strategy to position different beverages to different market groups. Keystone, for example, is popular and inexpensively-priced, while Coors Extra Gold is a premium beer that is more full-bodied.